A BETTER WAY
USING PURPOSEFUL TRUSTS TO PRESERVE VALUES & VALUABLES IN PERPETUITY

By Monroe M. Diefendorf, Jr.

A BETTER WAY

USING PURPOSEFUL TRUSTS TO PRESERVE
VALUES & VALUABLES IN PERPETUITY

MONROE M. DIEFENDORF, JR.

3 Dimensional Wealth™ is a trademark of The Foundation for the Encouragement & Preservation of Family Values, LLC
Certified 3 Dimensional Wealth Practitioner and C3DWP are certification marks of 3 Dimensional Wealth™ International, LLC

ISBN-13: 978-1493761715
ISBN-10: 1493761714
First Edition

Submit all requests for reprinting to:
3 Dimensional Wealth Publishing
Locust Valley, NY

Published in the United States by:
3 Dimensional Wealth Publishing
Locust Valley, NY

Layout by ABCMediaSolutions.com
Book cover design by Alex Mason

I would like to dedicate this book to all who seek to capture, protect, and preserve their family values; to those individuals whose concern for their heirs allows them to abandon traditional planning in favor of values-based planning; and to those whose unselfish love for their children and grandchildren allows them to look beyond themselves and well into the 22nd century by utilizing purposeful trusts.

Contents

Acknowledgments

I believe that we are who we are based upon all of the interactions that we have with the people who surround us. It is easy to identify these individuals in my life.

Monroe Diefendorf, Sr. – I attribute all of the values that I have to my father's upbringing. Having the opportunity to work with my dad throughout my life, I got to see servant leadership in action. My dad helped me understand how important it is to be worthy of your heritage.

Christine Diefendorf – My wife has been the love of my life. It has been my job to make the living and she makes the living worthwhile.

Ashley, Jennie, Whitney and Emily – It has been my hope that the values that were instilled in me would be passed on to my children. These girls (now women) have become everything that one would want a child to become.

Greer Kendall – In 2002, I met Greer who helped me articulate wealth in three dimensions. Without his prodding, I would not have written the book "3 Dimensional Wealth" causing me to re-engineer our financial wealth management firm.

Robb Musgrave – I met Robb after giving a speech in Denver, and it was as if we were reunited twins who separated at birth. Without Robb's work in developing "Valgenics," I believe that creating values-based trusts would be random vs. strategic in results.

Isabel Miranda – Without the guidance of an attorney who "gets it," I might still be trying to have values-based language created. Isabel was our lead attorney in the creation of Argonne Trust.

John A. Warnick – If there is a movement afoot in values-based (purposeful) trusts, it is due to the efforts of this man. It has been my pleasure to be a chartered member of the Purposeful Planning Institute.

JoAnn Dickinson – I am thankful that an experienced South Dakota attorney and trust officer was willing to take a chance on a very new trust company by becoming our Chief Trust Officer.

FORWARD

As a trustee of the John Templeton Foundation, I have come to appreciate that wealth management is more than money. And no one understands this better than Roey Diefendorf.

From his last book—that redefined wealth into three dimensions—to now developing strategies that turn his theory into practice, Roey is truly the innovative "thought leader" and pioneer in this arena.

Roey is to me, and to all who know him, a good role model who lives the song he sings about. It is a song of human flourishing for those who *give* as well as for those who *receive*, a song of faith in the ways and power of visionary love, a song of deeper purpose, and a song of abiding joy in contributing to the lives of others.

My advice is to throw away your preconceived ideas and traditional thinking as it relates to trusts and estate planning. As you read through the pages of this book, be open to the refreshing and profound message that transcends throughout. This is truly more than a new paradigm for managing wealth. It provides the framework for raising emotionally healthy and productive prodigy by providing a framework for *empowerment* rather than *entitlement*.

The long-term effects of Roey's work will not be fully appreciated during his lifetime, as this is 22nd century "stuff." It is said that societies grow strong when old men plant trees whose shade they will never sit under. Kudos, Roey, for your groundbreaking work.

Finally, this is not just an informational book but a transformational process that I believe families of "every day wealth" can and should embrace and incorporate into their "total" wealth planning.

May you be inspired by the wisdom and practicality of each page to "go and do likewise."

Stephen G. Post, PhD

About the Author

Monroe "Roey" Diefendorf, Jr. is a true visionary and pioneer in the total wealth management arena. He began selling life insurance before he graduated from high school and now, 43 years later, he has accumulated professional designation in life insurance, financial planning, investment management and philanthropy. As life-long learner, he has been able to assimilate all disciplines into his 3 dimensional approach to wealth.

Roey's entrepreneurial spirit has led him to create his own broker dealer, registered investment advisory firm, tax preparation company, third party pension administration firm, insurance and employee benefits company, a fee-based financial planning firm, and a South Dakota trust company.

Roey is a man who believes it is important to "walk the talk." Hence, he has transferred 100% of his family businesses into his values-based dynasty trusts.

Throughout the decades, Roey has been a sought-after speaker, highlighted by his 2008 appearance with his daughter, Emily, before a group of 8,400 members of the Million Dollar Round Table in Toronto.

In addition, Roey has been the recipient of several industry awards.

- 2001 – Winner of the Fleet Bank Small Business Leadership Award
- 2005 – Finalist in New York Enterprise Report Small Business Award
- 2006 – Semi-Finalist in the Ernst & Young Entrepreneur of the Year
- 2009 – "50 Around 50" Award from LI Business News
- 2010 – Winner for the Northern Hemisphere – CRM Excellence Award for Efficiency from Gartner & 1:1 Media

The past is the prologue. Be assured that Roey's work has just begun. Having determined that there is a better way to structure one's wealth transfer (3 dimensional wealth), he is committed to helping families perpetuate their *values*, as well as their *valuables*, in perpetuity.

Nothing is more powerful than a man on a mission and this dynamo is just getting started.

Introduction

After thirty years of providing clients with an array of financial products and services spanning the entire wealth spectrum, it became quite clear to me that the answers we provided were (unfortunately) not effectively addressing the questions our clients were asking. Traditional thinking trains us to believe that the ultimate goal is to help clients create, grow, and perpetuate financial wealth. Our clients share in this thinking: as financial "partners" in the process, they expect us to create, grow and perpetuate their financial wealth, and if we can help them accomplish this goal, both client and advisor should prosper—this has been the prevailing expectation. In effect, however, this process is a *one-dimensional approach* to financial services.

Being a great-grandson in a multi-generational financial services business, I have witnessed the results our family has achieved working with clients across four generations. After a lifetime of service in this capacity, I have realized results that are quite different than what I was told would make our clients—and me—successful.

The truth is that financial success, in the traditional sense, does not equate to significance. In fact, financial success often turns out to be more *hurtful* than *helpful* to a family's well being: possessing more valuables becomes the problem, not the solution. And here I was for much of my career (along with many, if not most, other financial advisors) adding more fuel to the fire by working on strategies and techniques to create, grow, and perpetuate a client's financial wealth.

Having read Bob Buford's book, *Halftime: Moving from Success to Significance*, in 1995, I realized that I was experiencing my halftime epiphany. Having played the financial services game for 30 years (hopefully only the first half of my life), I found myself in the proverbial locker room at half-time, pondering the question:

Am I going to play the second half the same way I played the first half?

And my answer was "No." I could not continue to follow the traditional trajectory of a financial advisor's career: providing answers that delivered only half-baked solutions. It was time to redefine wealth, and for me, this was the birth of an entirely new way of thinking, something I call "3 Dimensional Wealth."

3 Dimensional Wealth, the book, was published in 2005. It presents a radically new—yet sane—approach to wealth management. In my new way of thinking, wealth is comprised of three components instead of one: first, a person's "personal wealth" – *who they are*, second, their "financial wealth" – *what they have*, and third, their "social wealth" – *how they can make a difference*.

My hypothesis could be stated as follows:

> By managing one's "total" wealth, i.e. in all three dimensions, it is possible to transform a life of mere financial success into a life of significance.

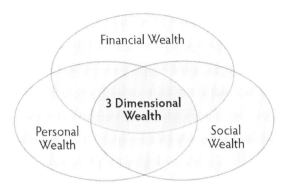

And so the journey began…

As a pioneer in this new way of thinking, I found myself virtually alone in the total wealth management arena, with hardly any trailblazers to follow. I knew my journey would be shorter and far simpler if I walked the well-worn path followed by the traditional advisors, yet I had no path, and this at first concerned me. But once I got started on my journey, and more importantly once I got a glimpse of what the future held in wealth management—with a 3 Dimensional Wealth perspective—there was no turning back. I couldn't. I wouldn't.

What would it take for me to make this journey?

Total independence. I would need to create my own broker-dealer. Since I was traveling in a direction opposite to that of the more traditional forms of financial services, by having my own broker-dealer I could avoid being stalled by compliance issues. In other words, I would need to make a financial investment that I most surely would never live long enough to capitalize on. It also meant I would likely spend the remainder of my career searching for ways to execute a total wealth plan—a 3 Dimensional Wealth plan. In essence, I concluded that perpetuating *values* was more important than perpetuating *valuables*.

Yet, how was I to accomplish this task with the limited financial tools I held in my toolkit?

My search began—and ended when I discovered the South Dakota dynasty trust. This was the missing link, and I added it to my arsenal. Hence, Argonne Trust Company was born. Chartered by the Division of Banking in South Dakota on March 29, 2012, we now had the necessary tools to administer purposeful trusts, also known as "values-based trusts."

Finally, I had discovered *a better way,* and my journey started. Now, in retrospect, I hope that by reading these pages you too can share in this journey and that ultimately you also will benefit from the power inherent in values-based trusts.

Monroe M. "Roey" Diefendorf, Jr.

1

PHISSION™: THE EXPLOSIVE POWER FROM SPLITTING AN ASSET

In 1944, Otto Hahn received the Nobel Peace Prize in Chemistry for discovering *nuclear fission*, the explosive release of energy that follows the splitting of an atom. The amount of energy released in nuclear fission is so powerful it can destroy entire cities—or power them.

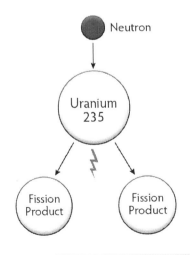

Fission: The splitting of a nucleus of an atom

In 2011, Roey Diefendorf coined the word, "Phission™," which, in a similar fashion, is the phenomenon that results when an asset is split into two parts: (1) the "Title to" an asset and (2) the "Enjoyment of" an asset.

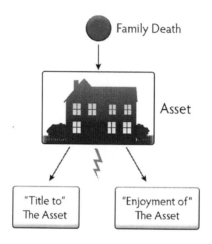

Phission™- The splitting of an asset into two parts

The power that can be generated from the use of Phission™ becomes evident when utilizing a dynasty trust in one's estate planning. Phission™ represents a new type of estate planning that departs from the traditional way of thinking.

With traditional estate planning, the assets are often divided equally and "left" to the heirs (i.e. children). The heirs are ultimately given title to the assets, and they assume the ownership of the asset. With ownership goes all the advantages and disadvantages associated with the asset. The drawback is that once the heirs take title to the assets, they are then subject to the "detractors" that go hand-in-hand with asset ownership, like divorce, lawsuits, squandering, taxes, etc.

Asset Ownership: "Title to" versus "Enjoyment of"

By implementing the Phission™ concept using a South Dakota dynasty trust, it becomes possible to break the asset ownership into two parts:

1) "Title to" the asset

2) "Enjoyment of" the asset

The title to the asset remains in the name of the dynasty trust, with absolutely no technical ownership at all by the family, yet the family retains all the rights to use the asset, in perpetuity. Think of it this way: if the asset in question is a house, then the title to the house is put in the name of the trust, and although none of the heirs *owns* the house per se, all of them can continue to *use* the house.

You might visualize this concept as follows: Suppose a grandfather homesteaded in America many years ago and built a small cabin. The original structure remains in its earlier form, but over the years various additions have been made to the structure and the property has not only increased in size and complexity, but it also has quite a bit of family history behind it. All the grandkids go there to spend time in the summer, and for other family events. Many things have taken place on the property and now it evokes a certain "feeling," not only for the granddad, but also for the children and grandchildren. Some family members even say, "Whenever I get near the place, my whole attitude changes for the better."

The grandfather wishes to capture and preserve this feeling— this positive effect on the family—and he wants to perpetuate this to his descendants. This is not about taxes, or property valuation, or some other tangible item; rather, it is about "family unity" and passing on family values.

Definition
"Beneficiary"

noun
A person, or legal entity, that is eligible to receive a distribution from a trust, will or life insurance policy.

As another example, consider an apple orchard. If the ownership of the orchard is to be passed to several family members the traditional way, it is likely that the orchard would be sold off for money and then the money split up among the beneficiaries. If however, the title to the orchard is transferred into a dynasty trust (using the Phission™ concept), the orchard remains the property of the trust, and the beneficiaries—all of the family members—can continue to pick apples from the orchard, in perpetuity. In this fashion, all of the *disadvantages* of ownership are bypassed, while all of the *advantages* are retained.

Creditor proof! Divorce proof! Estate-tax free—forever!

South Dakota is unique in this respect: unlike most other states, it does not require a "named" (living person) as a beneficiary. The beneficiary can be a "family value" or a "special purpose" that the trust planners want to pass on in perpetuity. The list of possible *values* is virtually endless, and in South Dakota, the flexibility of the dynasty trust is virtually unlimited, too.

Here are some possibilities:

- Perpetuation of a family retreat (a compound)
- Incentive provisions for care of either children or elderly
- Family financing—by loan (as a bond) or by investment (as an equity)—for home purchase or business venture

This new way of thinking about estate planning can be difficult to comprehend at first. For most people, splitting an asset through Phission™ requires a paradigm shift from the old way of thinking about ownership ("title to") to the new way of thinking. This new way of treating ownership and assets ("enjoyment of") may be described better as a sort of stewardship.

Definition
"Stewardship"

noun
The protection of, and responsible overseeing of, something considered valuable and worth preserving.

Once this radical shift in thinking occurs, the floodgates open and many new and creative estate planning opportunities present themselves. With all of its flexibility and the many advantages, the South Dakota dynasty trust should become the central part of one's estate plan.

Besides the intangible benefits, there can be significant financial advantages to setting up a dynasty trust. The Mitt Romney Story *(see Appendix F)* is a dramatic example of that. He saved over $25 million (and growing).

2

WHAT IS A PURPOSEFUL TRUST?

A trust is an efficient and effective way to distribute assets, providing legal, tax, and investment management.

A *purposeful trust* (or values-based trust) is a type of trust without beneficiaries. Instead of the traditional structure, it exists for advancing some type of non-charitable purpose. A purposeful trust is not available everywhere. In most jurisdictions, such trusts are not enforceable outside of certain limited (and anomalous) exceptions. Some countries, including Bermuda, Isle of Man, and the Virgin Islands—along with the state of South Dakota—have enacted legislation specifically to promote the use of non-charitable purpose trusts.

A purposeful trust provides an opportunity to put one's "fingerprint" and "voice" on the document in a personalized way. It speaks to beneficiaries on an individual basis and is a vehicle to combat the negative psychological implications (common in the trust business) of "I didn't trust you." It is designed to give beneficiaries great opportunity and hope.

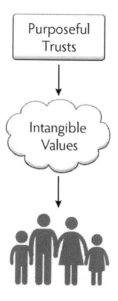

Unlike traditional trusts, which often are riddled with confusion and ambiguity, a purposeful trust is by its nature a clear and concise document, and thus it is more readable and far easier to understand. This type of trust is an effective way for the trust creator's true purpose and intent to be revealed. It illustrates one's beneficial reflections and life experiences, providing beneficiaries with words of wisdom.

Unlike a traditional trust, a purposeful trust is not an incentive-based trust that requires "acceptable" behavior for receiving trust benefits. Traditionally, these types of provisions have caused antagonistic feelings towards the grantor and trustees. In today's society, self-absorbed thinking and actions dominate the landscape. The goal of a purposeful trust is to provide the beneficiaries a platform for expressing appreciation and gratitude for what they receive. This is accomplished by capturing the *meaning* behind the gifts provided in the trust (rather than the financial *value*). In addition, the symbolic power of the naming of the trust can create positive emotions for both the grantor and the beneficiaries.

Definition
"Grantor"

noun
The person who creates the trust and places assets—
tangible or intangible—into the trust.

Traditional trusts define beneficiaries by name or by class (children/grandchildren). Purposeful trusts allow for the beneficiary to be a "purpose". A purpose might otherwise be described as a "value" for which the grantor wishes to perpetuate. For example; as grantor, I value the family as an important part of growing emotionally healthy children, hence, I seek to use my financial resources to promote family unity. This will be accomplished by providing full funding for an annual family reunion for those who are willing and able to attend.

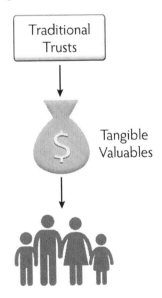

The grantor has no way of knowing who will actually participate in such an event, versus stating that each child will receive an equal amount of money to do with however they would like, which might be to attend a family reunion.

South Dakota has the only trust statues that allow a beneficiary to be a "purpose." One would have to go offshore to Bermuda, Isle of Man, or the Virgin Islands to get the same provisions. The significance is that rather than naming a person as a beneficiary to whom you will distribute assets, your assets can be distributed to maintain a purpose, a value, a principle.

As such, for many people, purposeful trusts are an attractive alternative to the traditional trust and are an effective mechanism to perpetuate values should one feel the need to do so. A purposeful trust hopefully can turn the planning process into a fun experience. The results of completing such a trust will project the grantor's life—in particular the values of the grantor—into the lives of the beneficiaries for generations to come.

Traditional Trusts	Purposeful Trusts
• Incentive-based	• Values-based
• Requires "acceptable" behavior	• Beneficiaries can be a "purpose"
• Limited duration	• Unique to South Dakota
• Beneficiaries by name or class	• Avoids "I didn't trust you" feelings
• Often ambiguous intent	• Allows for personalization
	• Clear and concise intent

In a purposeful trust, the grantor defines those values he or she wishes to perpetuate. As an example of conveying these values in writing, see *Appendix A – Letter to the Heirs.*

3

Why Create a Purposeful Trust?

While most choices are not as simple as black or white, allow me to suggest that attempting to perpetuate one's values is meaningful and purposeful. More often than not, leaving "valuables" (money or other physical assets) to heirs without leaving "values" (principles) will not produce the results most of us hope for—productive, well-adjusted prodigy. No, more money all too often IS NOT the correct answer (if ever!); rather, perpetuating *both* values and valuables seems to work the best.

When I began my career in wealth management, I was instructed to focus on the preservation of principal for the client's well-being. "Return OF the principal" was the mantra instead of "return ON the principal." We established trusts to protect and preserve. We did our planning based on the concept of the more principal we were able to pass to the kids, the better the estate plan. But that was then, and this is now.

The Importance of Principles

In the current day, our focus in planning for clients is significantly different. Yes, preservation of principal is still one of the goals; however, preservation of *principles* is the ultimate goal.

What does preservation of principles mean and how can it be accomplished?

Principles are the bedrock of society. Principles are what the United State was founded upon. The Bible, both Old and New Testaments, established principles by which to live. Without principles, we would be a lawless people and chaos would run rampant throughout the land. Without principles, individuals would be consumed by self-absorption, self-indulgence and our social structure would implode, perhaps like the boys did in the novel *Lord of the Flies*. Hence, establishing principles within a family is crucial to raising well-adjusted, productive progeny. So throughout our lives, as we raise our children, we instruct and model just what a principled life is and how to achieve peace and prosperity.

PRINCIPLES

If principles are as important as I claim they are, then to what extent would we endeavor to try and guarantee their perpetuation? We create elaborate schemes of all kinds in our efforts to perpetuate our *valuables* for our heirs but completely dismiss the notion of perpetuation of our *values*. And perhaps this is because there has been no tangible way to accomplish this objective. And why is this?

All the tools and techniques we have been taught, with respect to asset management, have existed within the realm of the *financial* dimension. And we do whatever we can to accumulate and build wealth, to create a legacy with the goal of making our children and grandchildren "better off" (financially, for the most part). But the paradox with "money wealth" is that the more you have, the less "personal wealth" you attain. I'm sure you can think of at least one real-life story about a person who has had more money than they could spend in a lifetime reach the end of their life only to find themselves broken, depressed, and despondent.

However, what if there was a way to capture and preserve one's values? What if there was a way to quantify and articulate these values? And what if in addition to merely passing on financial principal you could preserve your principles for unborn generations. This is my mission: to help my clients accomplish just this.

Not only is it important to preserve principles, it is also now possible to create a purposeful plan to accomplish this.

Living in an Inverted U-Shaped World

Malcolm Gladwell, in his book *David and Goliath,* reasons that we often overlook the obvious to make assumptions that ultimately prove to be incorrect. He uses the biblical story of David and Goliath, along with other examples, to show that unexpected—and often nontraditional—methods can be employed to overcome seemingly insurmountable odds. In the biblical story, David used a stone from his slingshot propelled at 150 miles per hour to strike Goliath in the forehead, dazing him enough to finish the battle at close quarters. Everyone believed small David had no chance against large Goliath—an expectation built on faulty reasoning. In this case, the slingshot is a nontraditional method used to overcome a seemingly overwhelming foe.

Gladwell shows that people in society have many preconceived expectations that are built on faulty reasoning. He relates the story of a California girls basketball team that uses a non-traditional method—a perpetual full-court press—to win against seemingly unbeatable teams and to achieve a "dream season."

Again, this is an example of an underdog using a nontraditional approach to solve a difficult problem and achieve an outcome that conflicts with societal expectations.

Gladwell also points out that society generally expects that having more money equates to happiness. However, with respect to raising well-adjusted children, he believes more money only brings happiness to a certain point. He makes reference to the research of Dr. James Grubman, who has studied the amount of "difficulty" involved in raising well-adjusted children in a wealthy family. Grubman's research indicates that "more is not always better" (going against societal expectations).

And why is this?

According to Grubman, it is due to the fact that we live in an *inverted U-shaped world.*

Gladwell describes an individual who struggles financially as he grows up. He comes from a family that closely watches how they spend every penny. He learns that the family must make value judgments about how to allocate resources. The impact of these struggles during his developmental years is seared into his attitude and behavior patterns. He thus learns the value of money and the virtue of independence and hard work. Yes, we all agree that money is necessary for a "better" life, so he seeks riches to make life easier for his children. Consider the graph in Figure 3-1, which is derived from a similar graph in *David and Goliath:*

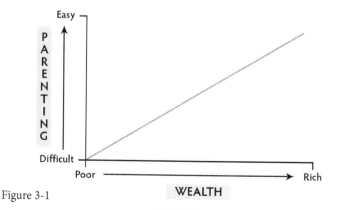

Figure 3-1

18

This represents the traditional way of thinking, i.e. that "the more money one has, the easier it will be to raise children." But according to the research of James Grubman, such thinking is based on incorrect data. In fact, the curve should not be linear at all; rather, it should be an inverted U. See Figure 3-2, also derived from David and Goliath, per the ideas of Dr. Grubman. This implies there is a point of diminishing returns—a point where wealth is no longer helpful and ironically becomes hurtful in raising children.

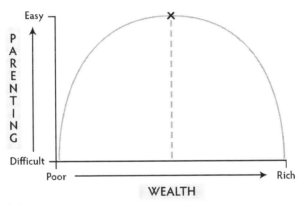

Figure 3-2

We can use the excellent work of Dr. Grubman, and the insight provided by Malcolm Gladwell in *David and Goliath* as a foundation to build on. According to Grubman, raising children gets more difficult when wealth reaches a certain level. Note that the scale of "difficulty" changes subtly here since the difficulty of not having enough money is different than the difficulty of having too much money. In the former, "difficulty" relates to the inability to provide food and shelter while in the latter, "difficulty" is a measure of something that relates to values (certainly not to an *excess* of food and shelter, the other extreme).

In any case, too much money does create difficulties, and this inverted U-shaped curve illustrates that traditional thinking about wealth creation only works to a certain point. Once one reaches the apex of the curve, "more becomes less." Grubman points out that a family with modest wealth and in the creation stage of their journey, can say "No, we can't" to their children due to lack of resources. However, a family with abundance cannot say "No, we can't" to their children based on a lack of resources; rather, they must say, "No, we *won't*," and this requires a *conversation* with children. Grubman writes that the children need to be taught this message: "Yes, I can buy that for you. But I choose not to. It's not consistent with our values," and this message requires that the parent has a set of values they can articulate and make plausible to the child—very difficult, as Grubman puts it, "under any circumstances and especially if you have a Ferrari in the driveway, a private jet, and a house in Beverly Hills the size of an airplane hangar."

This kind of planning—values-based planning via a purposeful trust—goes far beyond the traditional estate planning and wealth management. It requires that "values" becomes part of the conversation, not simply "valuables."

Based on my experience, I would suggest that in addition to the apex on the inverted U curve, there are two additional points that need to be addressed (see Figure 3-3). Point B is the point in time when the family realizes that (1) their abundance of wealth has become a problem and (2) that it takes away from the health and "total" wealth of the family. My experience indicates that when a situation reaches this point, it's usually too late— the damage has been done. Point A, on the other hand, occurs when the family has amassed enough wealth and there is still a positive effect on the family from creating more, but the positives come at a diminishing rate. This is the optimal time to initiate values-based planning. Although many would expect that such planning should begin at the apex, for maximum benefit, values-based planning should begin at point A.

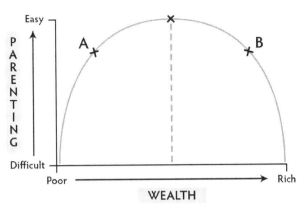

Figure 3-3

The strategies described in this book are designed to help you avoid the pitfalls of traditional planning, which all too often lead a family to point B. These strategies will help you plan and implement a new trajectory, one that will allow you to perpetuate values into the next generation. By protecting your values—i.e., by putting these values first (*before* your valuables, in contrast to traditional planning)—the inverted U-shaped curve becomes the curve you see in Figure 3-4, and the negative consequences are avoided.

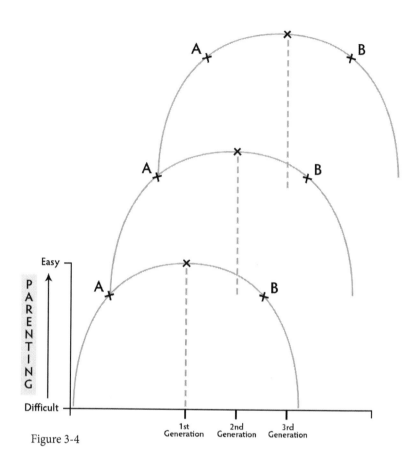

Figure 3-4

4

TRADITIONAL PLANNING VS. PURPOSEFUL PLANNING

Now consider the traditional planning process versus the purposeful planning process. Although the assets, in *both* cases, are ultimately removed from the decedent's estate and transferred to the beneficiaries, the impact this has on the heirs is significantly different.

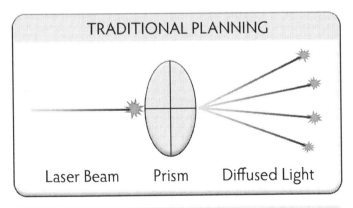

Resources and values get scattered / diffused

Figure 4-1

23

I see the traditional process similar to passing light through a prism. The light is diffused and the result is fractured light, or a rainbow. The intensity of the beam is minimized into numerous separate strands of differing colored light (Figure 4-1).

Contrast that to a laser beam, where the light is concentrated into a single focus. With enough intensity, light can actually cut through steel. Purposeful planning is a process that unifies the family resources and values so they can be perpetuated (Figure 4-2).

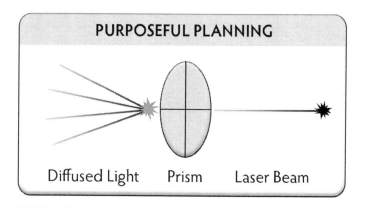

Figure 4-2

Traditional Planning

Traditional planning typically suggests that assets are distributed among heirs equally. Naturally, you have worked a lifetime creating your financial wealth and you want to preserve these valuables for your family. In essence, the traditional method *diffuses* the resources so each beneficiary has an equal but separate share. Each individual heir then works during his or her lifetime to increase that share, fighting off the various predators—taxes, litigation, and divorce—along the way. This process is perpetuated from generation to generation. And so the cycle continues: two steps forward, 1 step back.

But is there more to one's wealth than merely tangible assets and valuables—i.e., more than just financial wealth?

Purposeful Planning

Purposeful planning is the process of capturing and preserving your intangible assets and values—your *personal* and *social* wealth.

How is this accomplished?

The purposeful planning process is analogous to a laser beam in that it provides clarity and focus. Your core values are prioritized so that you understand which to protect and perpetuate for your heirs (Figure 4-3). Your financial resources are then structured to support the preservation of your values for generations to come.

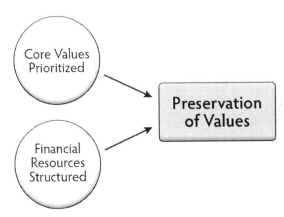

Figure 4-3

Fortunately, there are "total wealth" managers who understand the multiple-dimensionality of wealth and attorneys who embrace the "voice of the client" when drafting documents that capture the essence of the client's being and intent. And finally, there are trust companies that have statutes that allow for purposeful planning.

Having seen the financials of more than 10,000 clients during my career, I am totally convinced that a traditional distribution of assets to heirs without a "values wrapper" can do more harm than good. Only when a family addresses their "3 Dimensional Wealth"—personal, financial and social—can they go beyond success to significance (Figure 4-4).

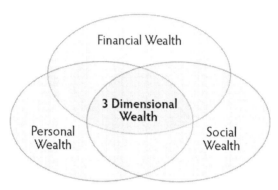

Figure 4-4

3 Dimensional Wealth

Financial Wealth

Financial wealth is a straightforward concept that most of us are already familiar with. It is the property we own, our assets, the amount of money we have in the bank. It is our net worth and the sum of our worldly goods.

Personal Wealth

To illustrate the concept of personal wealth, consider the following. "Relationally," you may decide to pursue two new personal friendships, or take a family vacation with your spouse and children, or spend a minimum of one weekend alone with your spouse. "Professionally," you want to be the best you can be in your occupation so you commit to continuing your education by taking a minimum of one course annually. All of these activities would increase your personal wealth.

Social Wealth

Social wealth is not as straightforward a concept. It is the dimension of your wealth that provides the outlet for helping others. It relates to philanthropy and making gestures to improve the general good of fellow humans. Rather than try to describe it in words, I have added a story that I believe illustrates social wealth very well. See *Appendix E* – "Emily's New Shoes."

Throw your prism away when it comes to planning the distribution of your wealth. Become a laser beam, focus your total wealth and create an impactful legacy that will last after the money is gone.

Function and Form

But when is a gift a *gift* and when is it a *transfer?* Unfortunately, many people use these terms interchangeably. However, the generational impact is significantly different based on how the transaction is structured. And I'm sad to say that in philanthropy, 90% of the transactions are *transfers* rather than *gifts*. Here's the issue:

An individual has a desire to "make a difference" through the transference of his or her wealth. Fortunately, there are a number of estate planning techniques, both charitable and non-charitable, that make such transactions tax efficient. Advisors analyze the situation and collectively and collaboratively a plan is outlined and executed. This is the "form" or tactics of the deal.

However, the "function"—i.e. the family's values—are rarely considered. Another thing that gets little or inadequate consideration is how the beneficiaries will react and adapt. This begs the question:

Will the transfer of wealth do more to help or harm future generations of the family?

The answer to this question depends on what is put first, form or function. Allow me to suggest that when form precedes function, the result is dysfunction. However, when form follows function, we find beneficiaries adaptive, resilient and emotionally balanced.

Form Precedes Function

When "trustafarians" (trust fund kids) were asked if their trust was a burden, 80% responded "yes." They went on to say they felt that the trust was an "alien" thing they had to "deal with." 50% felt they were merely a "tax deduction" and that the gifts from the trust had "nothing to do with them at all." It's no wonder Junior is not flourishing.

Being a fourth-generation advisor in our family business, I have enjoyed a multi-generational view of the many plans we have created for our clients. These transition plans, which often seem to be "dream plans" when originally conceived, all too often deteriorate into family nightmares that become more of a burden than a benefit, and through no fault of ours. Although we implement all of the traditional tools and techniques available to design the "perfect" plan, these plans repeatedly fail to achieve their intended goals. In hindsight, I now understand that we were actually part of the *problem* rather than the *solution*. These traditional planning methods hardly ever work.

As an example of what can happen, I will relate the details surrounding one of these unfortunate scenarios. A founder of a highly successful family business transferred ownership of his business—on paper, through a series of gifts—to four of his children without ever communicating that he had done so. These children had secretly become co-owners of the business. It was to be a pleasant surprise. One of our goals when we devised the plan was to eliminate the estate taxes on the business when the founder died, and we achieved this. However, when the children discovered they were the new owners of the business, they began to compete with each other for the top position in the company— the CEO title. Each wanted control, and after a drawn-out and highly disruptive battle, the children filed lawsuits against one another, and to this day they are not on speaking terms.

This story has a very sad ending: the founder worked hard his entire life to create a successful business, something valuable he could leave to his children, something positive in their lives, but it turned into something very negative. I knew him well, and I am confident that this end result—the bickering, distrust, and family infighting—was not what he wanted for his children.

Thoughtless Transfer - Focusing on Form

Form (Tactics of the Deal) ⟶ Function (Family Values) ⟶ Dysfunction

Form Follows Function

When form follows function, we find beneficiaries adaptive, resilient and emotionally balanced. I now realize the above story would have a very different ending if we had planned different-ly and given family values (function) a higher priority than the tactics of the deal (form). As advisors, we should have (1) spent time helping the father identify the family values he wanted to perpetuate, and (2) helped him communicate these values to the four children prior to his passing. Had that been the case, the family business would have become the mechanism to fund the perpetuation of these family values—rather than the seeds of demise for the family unit.

Traditional planning methods failed the family in the above story because the structure puts money first while ignoring family values. In contrast, purposeful trusts are structured such that form follows function. Values come first so the above nightmare is less likely to occur.

Mindful Transfer - Focusing on Function

Function → Form → Harmony
(Family Values) (Tactics of the Deal)

Converting "Thoughtless Transferors" into "Mindful Givers"

It's clear that thoughtless transferors focus on the form. Mindful givers focus on the function. Families with mindful givers become "legacy" families, while families with thoughtless transferors simply remain wealthy families.

But how does one transition into a legacy family?

First, let's consider the function of a family. How is it that a family will "function." Under what principles will a family operate? What values should be protected and preserved for a family? What is the governance that allows the family to integrate, increase in energy, and grow? Without the giver becoming "mindful," the family will disintegrate, diminish in energy, and entropy will exist. It is imperative that a family understands the values upon which its foundation is built, because, if a family doesn't stand for something, it stands for nothing (see Appendix A for a good example of mindful giving).

Valgenics

An online tool called "Valgenics" is available to help distill and synthesize the dominant values of your family, so that you have an outline to help define your "function."

You can access the Valgenics tool here:

www.valgenics.legenis.com

Values

What values might help define your function?

Think about the message for yet unborn grandchildren or great-grandchildren. Does your family value higher education, home ownership, entrepreneurship, or perhaps stay-at-home mothers, or time spent on community service? A family legacy can be structured to "empower" those values rather than simply have them be an "entitlement" for future generations.

Communication

Communication is next. How many stories have you heard about the family member who sends the annual gift tax exemption check at Christmas—without ever receiving a thank you note? What was once presumed a luxury becomes a necessity. Hence, it's rare to receive a thank you note come back once the gift becomes entitlement and not empowerment. Families rarely talk about money, much less the values that a family wishes to perpetuate with its money. Normally, the gift is about "the transferor" rather than the beneficiaries. Strategic giving or mindful giving considers the function first. This requires the family to interact. However, this is not normative. When the gift is about the *beneficiary* and not the *grantor*, it becomes a gift. When it is about the beneficiary, the mindful giver must be proactive in engaging the beneficiary into the conversation. Surely it's uncomfortable, but just as with exercise, without discomfort there is no growth.

Preparing for the Journey

Finally, it is important to understand that becoming a legacy family means preparing for a journey of over 100 years! Mindful givers understand that a functional family requires values to transcend the generations. They also understand that the appropriate "form" (strategies like a dynasty trust) does exist to allow for generational wealth to exist.

All of this requires "thought leadership" today. It requires re-engineering the status quo. It requires a new paradigm that will prevent your family from following the "shirt sleeves to shirt sleeves" syndrome. A "3 Dimensional" approach to wealth management can and will provide you with the tools you need to develop "function" first *and then* to institute "form," resulting in a legacy family.

5

MYTHS AND MISCONCEPTIONS

"The great enemy of truth is very often not the lie – deliberate, contrived and dishonest – but the myths – persistent, persuasive, and unrealistic. Too often we enjoy the comfort of opinion without the discomfort of thought." - John F. Kennedy, 35th US President

I have identified several beliefs and notions about trusts that can fit under the general heading of "Myths and Misconceptions." Here are a few of them:

- "All trusts are created equal."
- "Minimize the amount for the government and maximize the amount for the family."
- "Values-based trusts are a new concept."
- "The more you can give the kids, the better off they will be."
- "The higher the return, the better."
- "Charity begins at home."
- "Trusts are a good way to protect your children from

screwing things up."
- "Never give up control of your assets."
- "Why bother planning today when the rules are constantly changing."

The thinking embodied in these beliefs and notions represents traditional "wisdom" about trusts—misguided "wisdom." And while each of these statements is partially true, I believe that none of them properly addresses the best interests of a client and their family. These misconceptions share a common feature: *they lack a factual basis.*

Let's look a little closer at a few of these and try to sort fact from fiction. Hopefully we can dispel the misinformation so you are in the best position to properly evaluate them and form your own opinion.

Myth #1: "All trusts are created equal."

Reality: Nothing could be further from the truth. In New York, my state of residence, the trust statues are much more restrictive than those in South Dakota, where we own our trust company.

A New York trust that is irrevocable is inflexible. A New York trust company has total control over the assets placed into the trust, but modification or termination of the trust is impossible. Adding a grantor as a beneficiary in the future is inconceivable. Hence, placing assets into a vehicle with these restrictions is beyond the scope of one's vision.

In contrast, a South Dakota trust has flexibility. A South Dakota trust can be a "directed" trust where the direction of the trust is determined by the family through the appointment of investment and distribution committees. The trustee is administrative only. South Dakota allows for a trust protector to "supervise" the trust. In fact, a trust protector can modify and/or terminate the trust in the future. In addition, the trust protector can add a beneficiary class in the future (two years plus one day) that may include the grantor. All of this while removing the assets from the grips of litigation, estate taxes, and divorce.

Definition
"Trust Protector "

noun
A trust protector is a third party trusted advisor—maybe a close friend, relative, or business partner—with no ongoing fiduciary responsibilities, who assumes special powers over the trust or the trustee.

Myth 2: "Values-based trusts are a new concept."

Reality: Values-based trusts have existed for centuries. An example of this would be the Rothschild family in the late 1700's in Germany. Mayer Rothschild established a family trust to act as a family bank for his heirs. The trust was used to both educate and establish a work ethic while promoting family harmony and unity. He understood that leaving "valuables" (such as money) without leaving "values" (principles) to your heirs does not produce the results you are hoping for—productive, well-adjusted progeny. No, more money IS NOT the correct answer. Leaving *both* values and valuables works best and has been working for "legacy" families who employ purposeful trusts.

Myth 3: "Trusts are too expensive and for only the ultra and uber wealthy."

Reality: Technology is the great equalizer. The powerful tools that were once available only to the rich and famous are now within the reach of everyone with an Internet connection. Here are some tools:

1) Aggregation software to keep track of all the assets within a trust

2) Trust accounting software

3) *Office Anywhere* software that allows a trust company to be totally accessible via the Internet

4) Document preparation software

5) *Virtual Vault* software to store documents online

6) *3DW-TrustSmith.com* for creating and implementing South Dakota values-based dynasty trusts

The last tool is a proprietary solution I use in my own company.

Myth 4: "A trust is a way to rule from the grave."

Reality: Those who think that trusts are a way to restrict or modify a child's behavior have a distorted view. A well-constructed trust should not put the reins on your kids; rather, they should empower your kids to be all that they can be.

> SURGEON GENERAL'S WARNING: Long-term trusts may have damaging and corrosive impacts on beneficiaries. The emotional toxicity of trust instruments may lead to impaired lives, entitlement, irresponsibility, lack of initiative and self-esteem. You should not execute this document without carefully considering what you have done to avoid these negative outcomes in the lives of your children, grandchildren and other loved ones.[1]

With the ongoing demise of the nuclear family, as well as the extended family, it becomes more difficult to create both a family identity along with family unity. However, the more stability one can introduce into a family, the "healthier" the children and grandchildren are.

Many families feel that to compensate for the emotional instability that exists, money and "things" are the answer. However, my experience has shown that these "valuables" exacerbate the problem. Unless these valuables are wrapped in "values," this approach is doomed.

---

[1] This Surgeon General's Warning box first appeared in The Purposeful Trust Handbook by John A. Warnick, for which credit is given.

Myth 5: "Dynasty trusts are risky."

Reality: The South Dakota state statutes and trust laws clearly provide for all of the provisions we are discussing. In fact, planning without a dynasty trust is risky. Consider this: Is there a way to maintain control of your business without maintaining ownership? How can you eliminate the risk factors that threaten the transfer to the next generation? What happens when shares get in the hands of in-laws headed for divorce? Does the thought of litigation haunt you because your closely-held business is vulnerable to claims of creditors? Yes, there is a better way: consider a dynasty trust holding your closely-held stock.

What does that look like?

A dynasty trust is an irrevocable trust that is never subject to estate taxes—in perpetuity. This trust can own all types of assets, including shares of a closely-held business. So the shares, in part or in whole, can be transferred into your dynasty trust. The business ownership is in the name of your trust with a South Dakota non-depository bank acting as trustee. This will remove this asset from your federal taxable estate. However, the day-to-day operations, along with employment and compensation decisions, will be under the jurisdiction of the management team of the company. Hence, the former individual shareholder can continue his/her salary and benefits, without having to have ownership of the stock.

Myth 6: "The IRS is looking into dynasty trusts and is going to be coming down on them. They are going to be legislated out."

Reality: One thing I am confident of is that there is no such thing as permanence when it comes to our tax code. Changes will be forthcoming, so get used to it. However, there is precedence for "grandfathering" laws which have been on the books and modified in the future. We believe that this historical approach to change will apply should modifications be made to dynasty trusts in the future. While there are tax benefits to having a South Dakota trust, and more specifically a perpetual, dynasty trust, there is nothing illegal about using them. When the rules keep changing, it becomes difficult to plan. But you must play the cards you are dealt. Those who fail to act—waiting for the movement to cease—will never act. And my experience has shown me that inaction is worse than action, even when the action taken may need to be changed in the future.

Myth 7: "You must pay a large trustee fee for the trustee to do nothing."

Reality: Being a corporate trustee has significant duties and responsibilities that justify trustee fees.

Potential clients for my trust company have asked their advisors (CPAs & attorneys) to review our proposal for establishing and administering their dynasty trust. I have heard these exact words before:

> "That fee seems awfully high. They really don't do anything after the first year. I'm named trustee on a client's trust and I don't do anything."

Yes. I too am named trustee on a few New York trusts, and I also do "nothing." But being a corporate trustee in South Dakota is a significantly different endeavor. Here's why (I'm drawing on my own experience with Argonne Trust Company):

1) As a corporate trust company, we come under the jurisdiction of the South Dakota Division of Banking. The requirements for obtaining and maintaining your trust charter are extensive. And as part of the ongoing process, we are subject to a two-week audit (that we pay for directly to the Division of Banking for their field work) to review each and every trust in our portfolio.

2) The Division of Banking requires us to maintain $500,000 of capital on deposit as a reserve, with an additional

$1,000,000 available, if necessary, to cover potential liability exposure.

3) The Division of Banking requires $1,000,000 of Errors and Omissions coverage for our seven trust marketing officers and chief trust officer.

4) An independent audit is also required annually in preparation for the Division of Banking's audit.

5) We must adhere to the 136-page Trust Policy Manual covering 65 sections of the law.

6) In order to have your trust to receive the benefits of South Dakota law, we must maintain an office (currently in Dell Rapids, South Dakota) along with a local attorney/trust officer to handle the fiduciary work.

7) We are required to pay an asset-based tax to the Division of Banking in South Dakota based on the value of your trust.

8) The Division of Banking requires that two of our board meetings be held in South Dakota to maintain our South Dakota situs for your trust.

9) All of our Trust Marketing Officers must be Registered Fiduciaries, and operate under the guidelines for fiduciaries.

Definition
"Situs"

noun
the situs of a trust is the location from which the trustee manages the trust.

All of the above are necessary for you to have a trust in South Dakota. And let me just say that all trusts are not created equal. There are numerous distinctions between a New York trust and a South Dakota trust. So if you are told, "We'll just do a New York trust; it's simpler," you are losing significant benefits afforded through South Dakota.

The following requirements are necessary to run the day-to-day and month-to-month fiduciary operations of your trust. Again, I will give you the requirements from my company's perspective.

10) We not only act as the administrative trustee, but often as a member of the investment committee and distribution committee.

11) We are required to review each trust monthly at our board meetings and keep the minutes (even if there is a "no action").

12) We must maintain a trust money market account which will receive trust income and contributions and from which trust expenditures and distributions will be disbursed.

13) We handle required/discretionary distributions pursuant to the trust's terms.

14) We must maintain storage of tangible personalty and evidence of intangible trust property (i.e. certificates of LLCs).

15) We must maintain trust records and submit them to the regulators at each audit.

16) We originate, facilitate, and review trust accountings, reports and other communications with the grantor and trustees, beneficiaries, and unrelated third parties.

17) We respond to inquiries from the grantor, trustees, beneficiaries and third parties concerning any trust created hereunder.

18) We execute documents (at the direction of the Investment Committee) with respect to trust investment transactions.

19) We make payment on installment obligations, if required (one payment—interest and/or principal—annually per obligation).

20) Preparation of a fiduciary tax return is included as part of the ACT fee.

Having said all of that, we charge a subscription fee (one-time) to establish the trust in South Dakota, a base annual fee for maintaining the trust situs in South Dakota, and an annual fiduciary fee for running the plan in South Dakota and preparing the fiduciary trust tax return. In summary, our fees are on average 35% to 45% less than those of our peers.

Myth 8: Values-based dynasty trusts take a very long time to create."

Reality: Technology has made this untrue. In fact, for Argonne Trust Company, we have developed 3DW-TrustSmith.com for creating and implementing a South Dakota values-based dynasty trust. See *Appendix D* for details on using 3DW-TrustSmith.com. Trust me: it becomes a very simple process when the right tools are available.

Myth 9: "I'm too old to have a trust. I can't afford to tie up my assets at my age. A trust will only benefit my children and grandchildren."

Reality: By creating and administering a trust in South Dakota, all of the traditional stumbling blocks are eliminated. Asset protection (from creditors and the government), without giving up the income, is paramount for a successful trust at an older age. Financial independence while you are living, and estate conservation, generation after generation, when you die.

Here's the paradox: The tighter one tries to hold onto their assets during life, the more of the assets they ultimately lose at death.

Myth 10: I do not have the time or knowledge to run my own trust."

Reality: Time is a precious commodity, but through the use of an "administrative" trustee, you can maintain a trust without the day-to-day management attention that might otherwise be required by using a personal trustee.

Myth 11: "If I put my assets in a trust, I will give up control."

Reality: Control/ownership *is* a myth. The truth is that all of us are merely "stewards" of our assets. You can benefit from them during your lifetime but ultimately when you pass away you pass the stewardship to someone else. I have found that the tighter one tries to hold onto their assets, the greater the anxiety they have by owning them. Here's the good news: as mentioned many times in the book (for emphasis), you can split an asset into two separate parts: (1) *title to* and (2) *enjoyment of.* Hence, you can transfer the title to an irrevocable trust while retaining the enjoyment of it.

Remember, any assets that you need to control by ownership will be taxed upon your death. This statement is not entirely 100% correct, however; it would be 100% correct if we were referring to a "delegated trust." South Dakota allows for a "directed trust" to exist.

Myth 12: "I cannot direct the investments within the trust."

Reality: Creating the trust as a "directed" trust (versus a delegated trust) in South Dakota provides for the family to "direct" the trustee though the establishment of two committees: (1) an Investment Committee and (2) a Distribution Committee. The Investment Committee determines how the assets within the trust are managed. They make the decisions when assets (closely-held businesses, real estate and/or investment portfolios) are to be bought or sold. They determine the asset allocation targets for the Investment Policy Statement. The Distribution Committee makes the request to the administrative trustee for payments to beneficiaries that comply with the wishes of the grantor. Hence, the trustee is "powerless" by itself and merely follows directions.

Investment Committee	Distribution Committee
• Manage Assets » Buy » Sell • Set Asset Allocation Targets	• Beneficiary Payments

Myth 13: "Putting anything in an irrevocable vehicle is far too restrictive."

Reality: The statutes in South Dakota provide for the creation of a "trust protector." Only eleven states recognize the legal status of trust protectors, and only six states allow settlers to appoint and remove trust advisors and trust protectors. South Dakota falls within both these categories. South Dakota statute lists the following twelve powers that your personally selected trust protector may exercise, if authorized by the trust instrument:

1) Modify or amend the trust instrument to achieve favorable tax status or respond to changes in the Internal Revenue code, state law, or the rulings and regulations thereunder;

2) Increase or decrease the interests of any beneficiaries to the trust;

3) Modify the terms of any power of appointment granted by the trust. However, a modification or amendment may not grant a beneficial interest to any individual or class of individuals not specifically provided for under the trust instrument;

4) Remove and appoint a trustee, trust advisor, investment committee member, or distribution committee member;

5) Terminate the trust;

6) Veto or direct trust distributions;

7) Change the situs or governing law of the trust, or both;

8) Appoint a successor trust protector;

9) Interpret terms of the trust instrument at the request of the trustee;

10) Advise the trustee on matters concerning a beneficiary;

11) Amend or modify the trust instrument to take advantage of laws governing restraints on alienation, distribution of trust property, or the administration of the trust; and,

12) Provide direction regarding notification of qualified beneficiaries pursuant to § 55-2-13.

The bottom line is this: Irrevocable in South Dakota makes "tying up" assets no longer an issue.

Myth 14: "I can no longer use my existing attorney if I use your trust company."

Reality: No. This is generally not true. As an example, with my own company, we support the client's attorney with specimen documents to aid in drafting the trusts. In addition, all legal work is reviewed by a team of South Dakota lawyers to insure adherence with the South Dakota statues. To protect the client, all documents are approved by Argonne Trust Company's compliance arm before the trust is established.

Myth 15: "I have to relocate to remove my assets from my state of residence."

Reality: All too often, I have heard people say, "I am going to move to Florida, so that I can eliminate my New York estate taxes."

Unfortunately, when the relocation is completed, the grandchildren are left behind in New York; the family is fragmented as a result of the move, but the estate taxes are eliminated. This is what I call, "letting the tax tail wag the dog."

What if there was a way to have your assets relocate to South Dakota without you having to change your residence? This is what I call, "having your cake and eating it too."

Here's how it works. Let's start with your investment portfolio. By establishing a trust (dynasty or asset protection) in South Dakota, the assets are removed from your state of residence, thus eliminating your state's inheritance or estate taxes. In addition, should you establish a non-grantor trust; you will eliminate state income and capital gains taxes on undistributed gains. This is a "no-brainer."

What about your real estate? In order to have this asset class reside in a trust, it must be titled in an LLC or corporation. For real estate that is outside of your state of residence, it escapes the inheritance or estate taxes of your state.

Finally, for closely-held business entities operating in your state of residency, using trust ownership will only escape federal estate taxes. But for those businesses which are located outside your state, inheritance and estate taxes at the state level can be eliminated.

Definition
"Closely Held Business"

A company for which ownership and control is maintained by a certain number of individuals, and often within the same family—rather than by individuals in the general public.

So you stay home and send your portfolio, real estate, and business on a trip to South Dakota without any moving costs.

While there are likely many more myths and misconceptions regarding trusts, I hope that this discussion addresses some of the typical nonsense floating about the marketplace.

6

DOMICILE SELECTION:
OFFSHORE OR DOMESTIC?

When it comes to selecting a trust company, location is one of the most important factors to consider. Historically, the majority of trust companies have been established in international domiciles, or "offshore." Values-based trusts can be established in Bermuda, Isle of Man, and the Virgin Islands in the international arena.

However, now that South Dakota provides for purposeful trusts, a low-profile trust can be created *within* the continental US or "domestic" US. Having all of the best trust features within the states is what led me to charter my own trust company in South Dakota.

To maintain its position as a premier state for trust companies, more than a decade ago South Dakota established The Governor's Task Force on Trust Administration Review and Reform. The Task Force makes annual recommendations, which then find their way into legislation to modify South Dakota law. This process provides the most efficient and effective environment for trust administration and facilitates a timely response to ongoing innovation and evolution in fiduciary services.

Highlights of South Dakota's attractive features include:
1) No state income tax
2) South Dakota is second to none in the US including:
   » Unlimited duration (dynasty) trusts
   » The best privacy statute ("total seal")
   » The oldest and best asset protection statute (including LLCs and LPs)
   » Among the best decanting, remodeling and reformation statutes
   » The most unique special purpose trust provisions

Definition
"Total Seal"

Total Seal - Refers to the ability to seal all records in any lawsuit permanently. South Dakota is currently the only state providing this feature.

South Dakota House Bill 1045

House Bill 1045 was passed by both houses of the legislature and became effective July 1, 2012. House Bill 1045 contained 27 sections addressing a wide variety of issues, including types of trusts and types of trust companies. Here is a brief recap of some of the key provisions that impact the trust and asset protection work we are doing through Argonne Trust Company:

Section 4 – This section deals with decanting and adds a provision that when decanting property from one trust to another, the granting of a power of appointment to beneficiaries of the second trust is expressly provided. Previously, three other states had expressly provided this authority and now South Dakota does as well.

Definition

"Decanting"

When a trust is decanted, it is basically rewritten to make it a more flexible document.

Section 15 – Section 15 indicates that an investment trust advisor, while serving as an advisor to the trust, may have the power to vote any stock or stock interest owned by the trust or all additional powers authorized by the trust instrument.

Section 16 – This is one of the key provisions in the bill concerning asset protection trusts. This section shortens the South Dakota statute of limitations from three years to two years after the transfer is made. This matches Nevada as the shortest statute of limitations and reaffirms South Dakota as the top jurisdiction in the country for asset protection trusts.

Section 17 – Section 17 clarifies the "tacking" of South Dakota asset protection trusts. It adds a sentence that the date of transfer is deemed to have been made as of the time the property was originally transferred. Thus, if a trust was began in another state with a four-year statute of limitations for asset protection trusts, and was transferred to South Dakota two years later, the transfer would already be protected. This provision should allow some extensive asset protection planning in certain cases.

Definition

"Tacking"

The process whereby a trust that is in possession of property adds its period of possession to that of a prior possessor trust.

Section 18 – This section protects the trustee of an asset protection trust against "claw-back" claims regarding distributions made before notice of a claim was received by the trustee.

Section 25 – This section specifically provides that unless expressly otherwise provided by the terms of the governing instrument or court order, any trust administered in South Dakota shall have the laws of South Dakota governing its administration.

Definition
"Claw-back"
A term referring to the act of re-taking possession of various assets when certain conditions arise.

Section 26 – Section 26 indicates that no provision of a trust directing or authorizing the accumulation of trust income is invalid, under public policy.

As we can see, by utilizing a domestic domicile trust, both the complexity and expenses are substantially reduced, allowing "every-day wealth" to participate in and enjoy the benefits of purposeful trusts.

2nd Annual Dynasty Trust State Rankings Chart

Steve Oshins, Attorney at Oshins & Associates, LLC in Las Vegas, Nevada, published *The 2nd Annual Dynasty Trust State Rankings Chart.* In the chart, overall annual rankings are tabulated for each state based on various criteria.

Rank	State	Score
1	South Dakota	98
2	Alaska (Tied for 2nd)	95
2	Nevada (Tied for 2nd)	95
4	Tennessee	91
5	Ohio	89
6	Wyoming	87.5

Rank	State	Score
7	Delaware	79
8	New Hampshire	75
9	Illinois	74
19	Florida	62.5

Here are the criteria used in the ranking, and the respective weight assigned to each:

- Rule Against Perpetuities - 30%
- State Income Tax - 30%
- Third-Party Spendthrift Trust Provision Effective Against Divorcing Spouse/Child Support (Divorcing Spouse - 12.5%, Child Support - 2.5%)
- Domestic Asset Protection – 10%
- Decanting Statute – 7.5%
- Directed Trust Statute – 5%
- Reputation/Other Adjustments – 2.5%

7

Values-Based Plan Designs

This is where you, the grantor, get the chance to articulate what's most important and to provide a mechanism that will help assure that your values will be perpetuated. Just imagine that you are no longer able to pass your assets to your children or grandchildren by name. Pretend that it is illegal to leave assets to individuals. You can no longer state "whom" you want to benefit from your possessions.

What does this do to your thought process?

It forces you to eliminate the "who" and it introduces the "why" to help you determine how to pass on your valuables. How does this flesh itself out in your trust structure?

While you would like to have your beneficiaries (children & grandchildren) receive the benefits of your trust, you must now determine how they can receive benefits based on a set of principles. These principles will be spelled out in "values statements." These values statements will be supported by financial distributions based on acceptance of these values. So all your heirs will become beneficiaries and will receive their "fair share."

Your values are your own, but to give you two *values statement* examples, consider the following:

1) "Our family seeks to promote unity across the generations. We hope to accomplish this by promoting attendance at a family reunion held annually."

2) "We believe that helping others is beneficial to promoting healthy, well-adjusted family members. To encourage growth in this area, we will use our financial resources to perpetuate personal philanthropy."

Let's analyze these two statements. The family value identified in the first statement is family unity. This is translated into "purposeful" trust language. These principles can be perpetuated in perpetuity.

In the second statement, the value of being blessed by blessing others is identified. This can then be converted into purposeful language that gives the framework for how financial resources are to be distributed. Again, these values are what are to be passed on to heirs.

As we said at the beginning, these statements do not identify the individuals who are to be the beneficiaries; rather, these family values are established and can be funded by your dynasty trust. And your beneficiaries benefit "in kind" rather than "in cash." However, purposeful planning does not preclude beneficiaries from receiving cash distributions "just because."

Hence, black-and-white, all-or-none thinking is discouraged in developing your trusts. 50 shades of grey is more likely the outcome of the planning. But without the purposeful trust, you will get the traditional vanilla flavored trust. More flavors worked for Howard Johnsons, at least for a while. I'm confident that the outcome of purposeful planning will produce the precise flavor that you like most. Again, I refer you to *Appendix A* for a good example of writing out values.

Some families simply fail to address the situation until it's "too late." Others try to pass the title of the family compound to individuals hoping that it can be kept intact for generations to follow. However, the predators (divorce, litigation, taxes, and squander) that arise in the future make continuity improbable or impossible. Many turn to trusts as a better option, but even here several hurdles still exist for successful family unity.

Consider these issues:

1) Who shall be the trustee of a family trust? A family member? An individual friend of the family? A corporate bank?

2) Who are the beneficiaries of the trust? What are their names? Do they have named descendants?

3) How long will the trust be in existence? How long before it must be distributed?

Definition
"In Perpetuity"

noun
Indefinitely; essentially, forever.

These issues have plagued families simply because a typical trust cannot be a "purposeful" trust. By that I mean a type of trust that can be established for specific purposes and objectives, under the laws of certain jurisdictions such as South Dakota. The specific purpose may in fact be to protect and preserve family unity through the enjoyment of a family compound. No named beneficiaries are stated, other than perhaps heirs of the grantor. Ownership (title to the asset) no longer resides with an individual. Individual ownership of the asset is eliminated and replaced by stewardship of the asset. The resources (potential income) from the trust are used to maintain the compound rather than diluted through distribution to numerous heirs.

In addition to allowing for preservation of "values" through its purposeful statues, my company, Argonne Trust Company, provides a family other unique protection due to its South Dakota situs.

1) *Asset protection* – South Dakota provides the best shield against litigation:

   a) Self-settled Trust Statute with two-year fraudulent conveyance;

   b) Statue codifying that a discretionary interest in a trust is not a property right; and

   c) Sole remedy charging order protection for LLCs and LPs.

In addition, a "total seal" provides maximum privacy protection, where the family doesn't want family matters available to the public. Together these provisions make South Dakota the most favorable jurisdiction in the US for establishing a trust.

2) *Divorce protection* – South Dakota has a "floating spouse" provision, which eliminates the need for a prenuptial both now and for future generations. Only the current spouse can have enjoyment of trust assets. Upon separation from the family, the spouse "floats out" of the picture and the subsequent spouse "floats in."

3) *Tax reduction* – South Dakota has no taxes whatsoever (individual income tax, corporate tax, gift tax, sales tax, excise tax, property tax or estate tax). Hence, a non-grantor trust can afford handsome benefits for residents in highly taxed states, such as New York, New Jersey, and California.

4) *Unlimited duration* – South Dakota is one of a few states that provides for trusts to last "in perpetuity." (Delaware trusts may only last for 110 years for real estate.) That means there is never an estate tax to be levied when one generation dies off and the next generation takes over—forever.

All four of these benefits, in combination, make an Argonne dynasty trust truly the best suited mechanism for "keeping together what your family has put together."

8

Costs, Fees and the Importance of Transparency

Argonne Trust Company has completed a survey of competitor trust companies from various states. We found that our fees relative to our peers are approximately 35% to 45% lower. (See Figure 8-1).

	Argonne Trust / South Dakota			Argonne Trust Co. Discount Rate
Asset Value	Portfolio	Real Estate	Business	
$1,000,000	$6,000	$6,500	$7,000	22.77%
$2,000,000	$7,500	$8,500	$9,500	36.65%
$3,000,000	$9,000	$10,500	$12,000	42.99%
$4,000,000	$10,500	$12,500	$14,500	44.32%
$5,000,000	$12,000	$14,500	$17,000	45.25%
$6,000,000	$13,375	$16,250	$19,000	46.06%
$7,000,000	$14,750	$18,000	$21,000	46.33%
$8,000,000	$16,125	$19,750	$23,000	46.55%
$9,000,000	$17,500	$21,500	$25,000	46.73%

	Argonne Trust / South Dakota			Argonne Trust Co. Discount Rate
Asset Value	Portfolio	Real Estate	Business	
$10,000,000	$20,375	$23,250	$27,000	45.00%

Figure 8-1

The "Discount Rate" column represents the discount we offer in comparison to six other trust companies (from South Dakota, New Hampshire, Delaware, New Mexico, Georgia, and Nevada).

There are three elements to a trust company's fee schedule.

1) *Subscription Fee* – This is a one-time fee to establish the trust account within the jurisdiction.

2) *Base Fee* – This is typically a flat fee based upon the number of assets (LLC, portfolio, insurance, etc.) that make up the trust. When comparing fees between companies, be advised that some trust companies cover the tax preparation as part of their fee, while others do not.

3) *Fiduciary Fee* – This is an asset-based fee that varies by type of trust (delegated or directed), the asset (closely-held stock, real estate, portfolio, etc.), and the asset value. In states where the Department of Banking taxes trust companies, the fiduciary fee is used to pass through these taxes to the trust.

In order to gain total transparency, the more granular the information provided the better. Trust costs are directly related to trust functions and expenses. There should be no surprises with everything spelled out in the Service Agreement.

9

IT'S ALL IN THE NAME

Think about the time you probably spent laboring over what to name your child. For some (including my parents) this was easy—Jr., III, IV. Perhaps easy, but purposeful. Your intent was to honor your ancestors. On the other hand, those not so inclined had to ponder each syllable, each name (first and middle), massaging all possible combinations to arrive at just the right message or label to present to the world at the child's birth. Keep in mind: this is all done without ever having met the recipient of this carefully chosen name.

So, you want to set up a trust and you have to name it something. Here are some typical names I might see:

"The 4/26/2012 Trust for John Doe"
"The John Doe Irrevocable Trust dated 4/26/2012"

And maybe, if the attorney is creative, it will say something like this:

"The John Doe Irrevocable Family Trust dated 4/26/2012"

Think about it. This is *your* trust. Your way to take everything you have and distribute it to those you love most, and yet you take no time whatsoever crafting a special name for the impact you hope to make on those who will follow—and who will hear the name many times to come.

Contrast this sort of whimsical approach with taking the time, and making the effort, to produce a careful choice of words that depicts precisely why it is that this trust exists. We recommend that the trust name have at least two, or better yet, three distinct parts.

The first name should be: *who it is that is establishing the trust.* The middle name should be: *for whom this trust is established.* And finally, the last name should be: *the purpose of the trust*—what lasting impact you want to gift to your heirs. Just as it did when you named your child, the naming of your trust takes on significant meaning, especially if it is to last for generations, or in perpetuity.

Allow me to present some examples.

- The Johnson Family Stewardship Trust
- The Baker Family Empowerment Trust
- The Smith Family Entrepreneurship Incubator Trust
- The Jones Family Values Preservation Trust
- The Stern Family "Dare Mighty Things" Trust
- The Baker Launch Pad Trust
- The Barbara & Frank Wilson Total Wealth Transfer

Trust
- The Jones Family Spirituality Discovery Trust
- The Stewart "Roots & Wings" Trust
- The Williams Family Partnership Trust
- The Stein Family Bank Trust
- The Harris & Jones Family Heritage Trust
- The Dixon Family Builder Trust
- The Costello Preservation of Dignity Trust
- The Romano Family Enrichment & Betterment Trust
- The Green & Anderson Family Wealth Multiplier Trust
- The Demetrious Heirs Wealth Leverage Trust
- The Taylor Phission Trust
- The Smith Family 911 Trust

You get the idea. The trust name should tell the STORY—your STORY. The remainder of the document will indicate how and when the trustees distribute the assets. Obviously, this takes careful consideration as to the values you wish to perpetuate or the impact you hope to leave for the benefit of your heirs. It's much more than just leaving them money. Money left to heirs void of values often perpetuates valueless heirs.

Make sense?

Remember, have some fun with this. Be strategic. Be purposeful. But, be yourself, so the generations that follow will know who you were.

10

Planning Opportunities

O nce you begin to understand the power behind a South Dakota trust, the planning opportunities are extensive. Here are some to whet your appetite.

1) Business Succession Planning – Business value is exempt from death taxes
2) Life Insurance Ownership – Lowest premium tax in the US
3) "Incognito" Prenuptial – Heirs have "floating spouses" who have no rights to trust assets
4) Asset Protection – Creditor proof/total privacy
5) Family Values Preservation – Identify what is most important to you to pass on
6) Dynasty Duration – In perpetuity
7) Family Retreat Perpetuation – Eliminating individual ownership
8) Philanthropic Planning – Making a difference
9) Family Bank – Private mortgages/loans
10) Venture Capital Fund – Seed starter equity investor

11) Special Needs Trust – Care for the physically, emotionally, or mentally disabled

12) Farm Preservation Trust – Allowing a farm family to reap the harvest from the farm by eliminating transfer taxes from generation to generation

13) Charitable Remainder Trust – Personal retirement planning strategy

14) Non-Resident Alien – Foreign citizens with US citizen or Green Card children

15) Pre-Immigration Planning – Unlimited transfers into the US without transfer taxes via a self-settled trust prior to immigration

16) Deferred Onset Trust – An unfunded trust (not requiring current administration fees) that springs into being at some future date (i.e. when death occurs)

17) Education Funding – Grants or loans

18) Family Emergencies – Job loss subsidy, foreclosure bailout, medical expense subsidy

11

THE KEY COMPONENTS OF A VALUES-BASED TRUST

In this chapter I will introduce and explain the methodology we use to develop a values-based trust. After spending years working with the process manually, we have created and fine-tuned a method that uses extensive, full-featured, automated tools to facilitate the process of creating a values-based trust. Figure 11-1 illustrates the flow of this method.

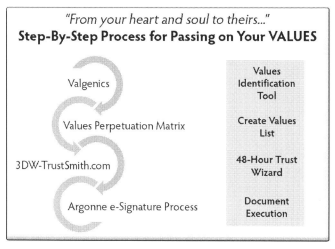

Figure 11-1

Values Identification through "Valgenics"

Valgenics® is developed by Valgenics® USA, LLC. To accomplish one's "total wealth" plan, Dr. Musgrave developed an online tool to synthesize one's values in only 20 minutes. This online values identification process is called Valgenics®. It starts with over 150 values sets and addresses the complex needs of individuals and families across all six value categories of life balance. It is these values that we use to develop the principles for perpetuation of values.

With even an introductory understanding of what a "values-based" plan can be, it is easy to see the immediate advantages in using this tool. Valgenics® has the following features:

- Establishes control and a sense of personal satisfaction
- Helps you define your purpose for a more fulfilling life
- Gives you security, generates confidence, and provides for your peace of mind
- Effectively communicates your personal values and beliefs to your family and loved ones
- Enhances your personal relationships, minimizing the potential for conflicts
- Maximizes your financial effectiveness and minimizes taxation
- Keeps all of your important documents together
- Ensures all your estate planning needs are met and remain current
- Provides innovative and sensible solutions that you understand
- Protects the inheritance of your family
- Establishes structured, charitable involvement to maximize the impact of your giving.

"The legacy we will leave is not just in our possessions, but in the quality of our lives." - Billy Graham

Values Articulation through the "Values Perpetuation Matrix"

This helpful tool provides a quick reference guide to give you practical suggestions for trust distribution methods based upon your values. It uses the following steps:

1) Identify the top three values (either personal or collectively as a family) from the Valgenics® exercise. For example; 1 – Spirituality; 2 – Education; 3 – Family.

2) Find the set of distribution possibilities that are related to your top three values. Read through them to determine if any of these suggestions would be the methodology that you would apply to you and your family. Check those that apply.

3) Next, rank from most important to least important of the selected distribution possibilities.

4) Finally, it's time to name your trust. Review the values you have selected and try to ensure the trust name reflects these values. Remember, this is the first thing your heirs will see as they review your trust.

By following these four simple steps, you are ready to move to the next phase, the *Trust Wizard.*

Values Trust Preparation via the Trust Wizard – "3DW–TrustSmith.com"

Based on your selections from the "Values Perpetuation Maxtrix," this phase will provide you with the legal language to incorporate into your trust document. Your document will be ready for your attorney's review within 48 hours.

For more details, visit www.3DW-TrustSmith.com.

Values Trust Execution through the "Argonne e-Signature" Process

Finally, though the latest technology, we can allow you to execute your trust document electronically in the most efficient way possible.

12

Successful Implementation and Administration

W e utilize a 7-Step transfer process when beginning a trust with Argonne Trust Company. See Figure 12-1.

Step 1	Creation of Trust Documents (see Chapter 11)
Step 2	Legal and Administrative Review
Step 3	Document and Transfer Preparation
Step 4	Trust Administration Committee
Step 5	Formal Notifications
Step 6	Asset Transfer
Step 7	Trust Administration Begins

Figure 12-1

Getting Started

Each new trust is assigned to one of our seven Argonne Trust Marketing Officers (TMOs), who will guide the trust through the 7-step onboarding process.

The most common reasons for beginning a trust are:

1) Elimination of estate/inheritance (federal & state) taxes
2) Elimination of state and local income taxes
3) Distribution of assets with a purpose

Once the decision has been made to establish a trust with Argonne Trust, the advisor and/or client will need to provide Argonne Trust with the trust documents and related information listed in Step 1.

The 7-Step Trust Creation Process

Step 1	Creation of Trust Documents (see Chapter 11)

Objective: The Trust Marketing Officer (TMO) is the lead contact during this stage of the onboarding process. In this step, the TMO ensures that the trust documents and related information listed below have been forwarded to Argonne Trust's Legal and Trust Administration group for review.

1) Information required for trust documents preparation:

   a) Personnel identified

     » Trust Protector (trusted advisor/non-family member)

     » Investment Committee (Registered Investment Advisor and/or family members)

     » Distribution Committee (Trust Company and/or family members—not beneficiaries)

   b) Written statement regarding the purpose of the trust and the current reliance of the grantor and/or beneficiary on the trust (distributions)

- » Discretionary Beneficiaries (by name)
- » HEMS (Health, Education, Maintenance, Support) Beneficiaries (by class)
- » Values-based Distributions (by purpose)
  - i. Family
  - ii. Education
  - iii. Financial
  - iv. Philanthropic
  - v. Spiritual
  - vi. Health

c) Trust document created with any and all amendments and court modifications

2) Required personal information:

- Information and status of grantor including: date of birth or death, occupation, citizenship, state/country of residence
- Information on all beneficiaries (current or remainder) including: date of birth, relationship to grantor, citizenship, occupation
- Information on all power holders or advisors identified in the trust including: relationship to grantor, citizenship, state/country of residence

3) If the trust contains an LLC, the following are required:

- Copy of any LLC agreements held by the trust or closely-held business interest
- Trust's ownership interest for any LLC in the trust or closely-held business interest
- Description of LLC assets and approximate value of property held by the LLC

4) If the trust contains any real estate, the following are

required:
- Full address or legal description of property
- Type of property—such as grantor/beneficiary residence, rental property, etc.

Step 2	Legal and Administrative Review

Objective: After receiving the above trust documentation and information, Argonne Trust's legal and administration groups will review the trust documents to:

> » *Determine whether Argonne Trust can administer the trust in accordance with its terms,*
> » *Identify any issues associated with the trust or the transfer of the trust to a successor trustee, and*
> » *Determine if all investments are acceptable.*

1) The TMO is responsible for compiling and organizing the information provided by the advisor. The TMO receives the trust documentation described in Step 1 and provides an initial review. If additional documentation or information is required, the financial advisor will be contacted.

2) The Argonne Trust Legal and Administrative teams review the trust documents to determine if the trust may be moved to a successor trustee and administered by Argonne Trust in accordance with the trust's terms.

3) Once the legal and administrative reviews are completed, the TMO will work with the advisor to resolve any issues identified during this initial review.

Step 3	Document and Transfer Preparation

Objective: With the legal, administrative and investment reviews completed, and all issues identified during the review resolved, signature-ready forms are issued to the financial advisor.

1) The TMO emails account-opening paperwork to the advisor, which the advisor and the client need to sign. The advisor mails the completed forms back to the TMO.

Note: The timing on completing this step can vary and depends solely on the advisor and his client.

Account-opening paperwork that the *client* will need to provide and sign:

- Removal and Appointment Document
- W-9
- Distribution Form
- Tax Preparation Directive
- Beneficiary Acknowledgment
- Advisor's Fee Schedule
- Valid Photo Identification

Sample account-opening paperwork the *advisor* will need to provide and sign:

- Broker Hire Agreement
- Delegation Agreement
- Investment Advisor Acknowledgment Form
- Investment Policy Statement

Step 4	Trust Administration Committee

Objective: The Trust Administrative Committee (TAC) reviews all relevant documentation and information, and based on the application of sound fiduciary standards, weighs the decision to accept the trust.

1) The TMO presents the trust to the TAC for formal acceptance.

2) TAC considers all comments and recommendations for assuming administration of the trust from the following

entities:

» The legal review
» The administrative review
» The Portfolio Analyst's review

Step 5	Formal Notifications

Objective: *Argonne Trust formally notifies the advisor and current trustee of Argonne Trust's acceptance of the trust. At this stage of the transfer process, the trust is handed-off to the Trust Administrator (TA). The TA becomes the lead contact for the advisor, grantor, and/or beneficiary and prior trustee.*

1) The TMO initiates the following communications:
   » Notifies the advisor of the trust's acceptance,
   » Introduces the TA to the advisor as the primary point of contact,
   » Overnights the trustee notifying them of their removal from the trust and that Argonne Trust has been appointed as successor trustee ,
   » This letter includes a copy of the Removal and Appointment document, Argonne Trust's formal acceptance, and a request for any additional items needed from the removed trustee, and
   » Initiates internal account opening process on Megethos3 (a system we use).
2) The TA will instruct the advisor to establish a brokerage account in the name of the trust, identifying Argonne Trust as trustee.

Step 6	Asset Transfer

Objective: *There are four steps associated with the actual transferring of the trust's assets:*

1) Identifying and valuating the Trust's assets prior to the transfer,

2) Transferring the trust's assets to the custodian,

3) Reconciling the assets after they have been transferred to the custodian, and

4) Funding of the "Cash Account" at Argonne Trust

When the account opening has been completed, Argonne Trust establishes a Cash Account to fund the administrative activities of the trust for up to a six-month period.

1) The Trust Administrator works with the financial advisor's office to prepare for the asset transfer:

   » The advisor establishes a brokerage account in the name of the trust, identifying Argonne Trust as Trustee (the completed application and forms are provided by Argonne Trust).

   » The TA establishes the Albridge Custodial Data link between the brokerage account and Trust Accountant.

   » The TA works with the advisor to establish online access to the brokerage account.

   » The trust's assets are then transferred to the newly opened trust account.

2) The TA, in conjunction with the advisor's office, monitors the asset transfer.

3) After the assets are received into the brokerage account they are again identified and valued by the TA.

4) Once the trust's assets are reconciled by the TA, the advisor may begin managing the account.

5) The Trust Administrator works with the advisor to fund the Cash Account. The Cash Account is established to pay four to six months of known expenses and distributions for the trust (the Cash Account does not pay the financial

advisor's fees).

Step 7	Trust Administration Begins

1) With the trust and administrative duties transferred to Argonne Trust, the TA becomes the primary point of contact for the advisor and the trust's grantor and/or beneficiaries.

2) The TA sends a formal letter of introduction to the trust's grantor and/or beneficiary, providing contact information and a calendar of communications the client can expect to receive from Argonne Trust.

3) The TA creates a "virtual vault" and deposits all relevant documents for the client's (and trusted advisors) easy access and review.

13

What's Next?

If you're like most, you will want to run this trust planning process by (through) your current set of advisors. There are only three possible responses you will encounter.

1) That's a great idea.
2) I don't think this is a good idea.
3) I don't know enough about this.

My experience to date is that only one attorney was humble enough to admit he knew nothing about values-based trusts. One agreed it was a good idea but went back to his old way of thinking. And the remainder (over 50 in number) said that they had never heard of values-based/purposeful trusts and therefore it was *not* a good idea. Don't let that stop you from making the most meaningful, total wealth transfer decision of your life. Read on.

One of our Trust Marketing Officers will be glad to arrange an initial complimentary meeting at either our New York City or Long Island offices, or by webinar. At this first meeting, it would be most beneficial to have a copy of your wills/trusts and your financial statement available. We will set aside time for a 90-minute meeting, which should establish if we can be of help to you.

Remember, the best time to plant a tree is 20 years ago—or today. It takes family leadership to think generations into the future. Start today, it's up to you.

Appendix A – Letter to the Heirs

To my descendants and their Trustees, both living and those to be conceived and born in the future:

On the most basic level, the purpose of this dynasty trust is to further the pursuit of happiness by my descendants. I use the phrase the pursuit of happiness in the same way as our Founding Fathers used it in the Declaration of Independence. Neither they nor I were or are talking about acquiring more material goods or taking longer vacations but rather the sense of self-sufficiency that is derived from becoming self-reliant and financially sound, (financial wealth), having a sense of emotional, social, and mental competence, (personal wealth) and giving back to the community, (social wealth).

The assets in this dynasty trust will help make things more convenient for my descendants but it cannot make them happy. I believe that the family's financial wealth, including the money in this trust, should be viewed as a tool to support the growth of the family's real capital, which consists of the family members and their knowledge achieved through life experience and education. That is why I believe that travel, involvement in philanthropy and education to one's maximum potential are so important.

This dynasty trust is designed to provide my descendants with the opportunity for an introduction to and education in the capable and responsible ownership of wealth.

It is my goal and ongoing desire that each generation be prepared for financial independence. By this I mean, learning these eight principles and applying them to their lives;

1) The ability to live within one's means, i.e. managing spending consistent with one's level of income;

2) The ability to manage spending relative to income in a manner that would be consistent with being able to save a portion of income, as needed.

3) The ability to understand and manage credit and debt processes, leading to avoidance of excessive debt;

4) The ability to maintain reasonable accounting of one's financial resources;

5) The ability to understand and manage one's personal assets, either using basic investment procedures and principles for oneself or to delegate these actions and responsibilities to appropriate advisors;

6) The ability to generate income for spending needs, thus not being dependent on the resources in this dynasty trust;

7) The ability to use a portion of one's income and/or financial resources to support charitable activities of one's choosing; and

8) The ability to show initiative, engage in entrepre-

neurship, and demonstrate purposeful thought leadership.

Making mistakes with money is an important tool in learning to manage money. The beneficiary should be allowed to take reasonable risks with money. A goal is for the beneficiary to develop skills in risk assessment, risk capacity, and risk tolerance, as well as to learn from both success and failure. The Independent Trustee should allow the beneficiary to encounter the consequences of his or her decisions. The Independent Trustee may neither be held liable for poor decisions on the beneficiary's part, nor responsible for not having foreseen unanticipated consequences of their decisions.

Disagreements on the part of the beneficiary and the Independent Trustee should be seen as normal and an opportunity for learning by the beneficiaries. Both the beneficiaries and the Independent Trustee should approach conflicts with a desire for collaboration, mutual understanding, negotiation, and demonstration of mutual respect so that conflicts are accepted and resolved using the highest principles of human relationships.

Many conflicts between beneficiaries and trustees arise because the beneficiaries have never read and do not understand the trust. Each generation of my descendants should seek to educate their heirs and the beneficiaries are urged to learn about the terms of the dynasty trust and the respective rights and responsibilities of the beneficiaries and the Independent Trustee. The Independent Trustee is encouraged to retain consultants to assist the beneficiaries in understanding the dynasty trust and in developing the eight financial literacy skills described above. Such consultants may be retained to work directly with the beneficiaries, to provide advice and counsel for all heirs, as well as for the Guardians of any minor beneficiaries.

Among the issues that such education should include are the following;

i) Understanding our family mission statement and any letters from me and/or videos.

ii) The basics of modern financial theories of investment and the asset allocation of the trust.

iii) The basic of trust accounting, so that the beneficiaries will be able to read and have a reasonable basis to evaluate the accountings prepared by the trustees.

iv) Basic principles of trustee compensation, as well as compensation to all other regular advisors and consultants.

v) The importance of participating in educational sessions and becoming financially literate.

When providing educational programs for the beneficiaries, the Independent Trustee is to keep in mind that people learn in different ways and at different speeds. Various assessment programs exist which will help the Independent Trustee identify how my descendants learn and to make certain that information is provided to them in a manner tailored to their individual learning styles. Such assessment tools include those which help to identify how we receive, process, assimilate, store and use information, and career or vocational testing which help to identify the beneficiaries' unique individual talents and interests.

The cost of all such assessment tools shall be charged against the trust assets.

My desire is in no way to use our dynasty trust

as a tool to manipulate heirs behavior, but rather to promote and perpetuate values which I feel will benefit our family for generations to come.

With God's help, my wife, Chris and I will raise our children and our children's children to become productive, contributing members of society.

May you accept the purpose of this dynasty trust in the spirit with which it was created and benefit richly from its provisions.

With much love,

Monroe "Roey" Mechling Diefendorf, Jr.
Born February 7, 1952

Appendix B – CPA, Lawyer, or Financial Advisor Notes

You will have to help your client negotiate the vast array of trust options to determine the best states and provisions available to accomplish their planning needs. Here's a helpful tool you can use to narrow down the field:

1) US "Domestic" Trusts (50 states, including South Dakota)
2) Trust Protector States (25 states, including South Dakota)
3) Perpetual Dynasty Trust States (23 states, including South Dakota)
4) Domestic Asset Protection Trust States (11 states, including South Dakota)
5) Directed Trust States (10 states, including South Dakota)
6) Purposeful Values-based Trust State (South Dakota)

Each of these six features has true significance and provides substantial benefits for your client. To overlook any of these features would mean that your client would forfeit what is available in the marketplace today.

Allow Argonne Trust Company to help you help your client perpetuate your values and your valuables in perpetuity.

Appendix C – History and Key Court Rulings

While rules against perpetuity is important when differentiating between one jurisdiction and another, there are other important factors, including; 1) state and local tax laws; 2) modern trust laws, which provide future flexibility; 3) asset protection laws; and 4) how trust migration reduces a beneficiary's distribution interest when compared to other beneficiaries.

Rules Against Perpetuity

Under the common law Rules Against Perpetuity (RAP) adopted from British common law, an interest in trust must vest, if at all, within "a life in being, plus 21 years (plus a reasonable period for gestation)." Several States adopted the Uniform Statutory Rule Against Perpetuities (USRAP), which sets the duration of a trust to the greater of the RAP or 90 years. However, in 1983, South Dakota was the first state to abolish the common law rule against perpetuities. Now over twenty states have done something similar.

Murphy

In 1979, the TAX Court affirmed Wisconsin's method for

repealing its Rules Against Perpetuity (RAP). Known as the Murphy approach, this case provides for the complete repeal of the RAP and substitution of a more flexible, alternative vesting statues. Four states, including South Dakota, apply the Murphy case making them the leaders in dynasty trusts.

Limited POAs

IRC Section 2041(a)(3) prevents the abuse known as the "Delaware tax trap" which refers to the exercise of successive limited POAs over successive generations, thus allowing for a virtual perpetual trust without federal transfer taxes. Therefore, the use of limited POAs is generally reserved for beneficiaries and decedents who are ascertainable upon the creation of the trust to prevent the inadvertent violation of Section 20141(a)(3).

Change of Situs

The ability to change the situs of family trusts is important to affluent clients. Perhaps they want to change situs so their trust will be in a state with more lenient income tax laws or better asset protection laws. If considering a situs change, examine the wording of the trust provisions, including perpetuities language and the applicable law; look at the possible negative impact such a change would have on GST tax-exempt status of the trust and its effect on beneficiary rights.

Directed Trust Statutes

Such a statute permits the client to select an independent party or parties, typically designated as a co-trustee or trust advisor, to manage closely-held businesses, investment asset and insurance. This relieves the directed or administrative trustee from the duty to manage the trust assets. Such use of an independent party makes it possible for clients to hold closely-held interest and ongoing business interests in a trust without an administrative or directed trustee's interference. Directed trusts also provide more flexibility and control over asset allocation, concentration and selection of investment. Directed trust fees are typically lower to reflect that the trustee isn't liable for the trust's investment activities.

Trust Protector Statutes

Such a statue recognizes the authority and limitations of a person or entity that has been appointed as trust protector. A trust protector is any disinterested third party whose appointment is provided by the trust instrument. This provides greater flexibility for future generations as conditions change. The power of a trust protector is as provided in the governing instrument and under state law.

Reformation and Decanting Statutes

These statues permit a trust to be modified within certain parameters to better meet a family's needs. Historically, only judicial action could modify a trust. This process often required the consent of all the beneficiaries or a court-approved equitable deviation. In addition, a trustee might, under common law, have the power to make distributions of trust property to another trust, even one created by that trustee. South Dakota's decanting stature, effective July 1, 2007, provides the best example of flexibility for trust remodeling.

Trustees or beneficiaries might wish to modify an irrevocable trust to:

1) Improve the trust's governance structure,
2) Change the law applicable to the trust when the terms of the trust don't facilitate a change to its governing law,
3) Change dispositive provisions,
4) Change the administrative terms of the trust to ensure that the trust provides the proper tools to its fiduciaries for the best management of the trust, or
5) Modernize an outdated trust agreement.

Special-Purpose Statutes

Special-purpose entities are intended to limit the liability of trust protectors, trust advisors, and investment and distribution committees. These entities are typically limited liability companies (LLCs) organized under the laws of a jurisdiction that permits the special purposes. They provide legal continuity beyond any single individual's death, disability, or resignation. Six jurisdictions permit special-purpose entities, including South Dakota.

Virtual Representation Statutes

These statues are designed to facilitate the administration and court supervision of a trust in which there are contingent, unborn, or unascertainable beneficiaries. Typically, if there is not a person "in being" or ascertained to have the same or similar interests, it's necessary to appoint a guardian ad litem to accept service of process and to protect such interests. Nine jurisdictions have virtual representation, including South Dakota.

Asset Protection

The asset protection planning key is to draft a discretionary trust in which the beneficiary doesn't have an enforceable right to distribution.

General Powers of Appointment

The strongest asset protection class of the truly perpetual jurisdictions include South Dakota, Alaska, and Delaware. South Dakota's SB98 affirmatively rejects the UTC and Restatement Third position by codifying common law. SB 98 Section 3 paragraphs (1); (2); and (3) provide that a power of appointment may not be judicially foreclosed, no creditor may attach a power of appointment, and a power of appointment is not a property interest.

Dominion and Control Arguments

Under common law, if a beneficiary has too much control over a trust a creditor may reach the beneficiary's interest. South Dakota's SB98 negates the Restatement (Third) Section 60 g. and cures the possible expansion of dominion and control arguments with the following provisions:

Section 5 states, "No creditor may attach, exercise, or otherwise reach an interest of a beneficiary of any other person who holds an unconditional or conditional removal or replacement power over a trustee."

Section 5 further states. "No creditor may reach an interest of a beneficiary who is also a trustee or co-trustee, or otherwise compel a distribution because the beneficiary is then serving as a trustee or a co-trustee. No trust may foreclose against such interest."

Section 9 states, "In the event that a party challengers a settlor or beneficiary's influence over a trust, none of the following factors, alone or in combination may be considered dominion and control over a trust;

- A beneficiary serving as a trustee or co-trustee as described in Section 5 of this Act;
- The settlor or a beneficiary holds an unrestricted power to remove or replace a trustee;
- The settlor or a beneficiary is a trust administrator, a general partner of a partnership, a manager of a limited liability company, an officer of a corporation, or any other managerial function of any other type of entity, and part or all of the trust property consists of an interest in the entity;
- A person related by blood or adoption to a settlor or a beneficiary is appointed as trustee;
- A settlor's or a beneficiary's agent, accountant, attorney, financial advisor, or friend is appointed as a trustee; or

- A business associate is appointed trustee."

Discretionary Trust Protection

South Dakota SB98 paragraph (1) of Section 20 codifies common law and states that "a discretionary interest is neither a property interest nor an enforceable right. It is a mere expectancy."

In addition, under common law the reason that a beneficiary of a common law discretionary trust did not have an enforceable right to a distribution (and therefore not creditor can stand in the beneficiary's shoes) was the limited judicial review standard for a discretionary trust. Hence paragraph (3) of Section 20 retains the Scott on Trusts categories for limited judicial review by a court for only 1) dishonesty; 2) improper motive; and 3) failure to use the trustee's judgment.

Alter Ego

Closely related to the concept of dominion and control is the doctrine of holding the trust as the alter ego of a settlor or a beneficiary. Following the approach of a DAPT statute, South Dakota law states:

"Notwithstanding any other provision of law, no action of any kind, including an action to enforce a judgment entered by a court or other body having adjudicative authority, may be brought at law or in equity for an attachment or other provisional remedy against property that is the subject of a South Dakota trust unless the settlor's transfer of property was made with the intent to defraud that specific creditor."

South Dakota statue says that the only remedy a creditor has against a South Dakota trust is a claim for fraudulent conveyance.

In addition, four states, including South Dakota have provisions stating that a court may not deem a settlor of an irrevocable trust to be the alter ego of the trustee even if the settlor has shown evidence of the dominion and control factors.

Spendthrift Protection

Spendthrift protection began in the United States in the late 1800s. Except for certain debts (such as child support, alimony, governmental claims or necessary expenses of a beneficiary) a spendthrift clause stops creditors from attaching the assets at the trust level and forcing a distribution.

Domestic Asset Protection Trust (Self Settled Trust)

Self-settled trusts are trust that settlors form for their own benefit. That is, the settlor is also a permissible beneficiary. Twelve states have self- settled trust legislation, including South Dakota.

Charging Order Protection

A charging order is a court order issued to a judgment creditor that forces an entity in which a debtor is a partner to make distributions to the creditor (rather than the debtor) until a debt is satisfied.

When evaluating state charging order statutes, we determined the best jurisdictions were those with a statue that: 1) prevents the judicial foreclosure sale of the partner's or member's interest; 2) provides either a provision denying any legal or equitable remedies against the partnership or a provision preventing a court from issuing a broad charging order interfering with the activities of the partnership.

South Dakota is one of the nine states that a charging order is the sole remedy, and there is no other language in the statue stating that a court may issue additional orders to effect the charging order or that a court may order the judicial foreclosure sale of the partner's or member's interest.

Migration

The migration of a trust from one jurisdiction to another can reduce a beneficiary's distribution interest when compared to other beneficiaries. Under the Restatement First, Restatement Second and most common law, if a trust instrument is silent on whether the trustee should look to a beneficiary's resources before making a distribution, a trustee does not have an obligation to look to a beneficiary's resource in determining the amount of a distribution. Unfortunately, the Restatement Third requires a trustee to look to a beneficiary's resources if the trust is silent. Currently, only three states, including South Dakota, have addressed this potential migration issue created by the Restatement Third by codifying the Restatement Second.

Summary of South Dakota trust statues:
- Rules Against Perpetuity (RAP) established 1983.
- Common Law Rule – Abolished
- Uniform Statuary Rule Against Perpetuities (USRAP) – No
- Murphy case applies – Yes
- Effective GST Tax Limit – Perpetual
- State Income Tax – None
- State Insurance Premium Tax – 8 bps
- Limited POA – URX Section 2041(a)(3)
- Change of Situs – Perpetual
- Directed Trust Statue – Yes
- Trust Protector Statue – Yes
- Reforming Statues – Yes
- Decanting Statues - Yes
- Special Purpose Entities – Yes
- Enhanced Virtual Representation – Yes
- Discretionary Trust Protection
  - » Not Enforceable Right – Yes
  - » Creditor Can Not Attach – Yes
  - » Second Judicial Review – Yes
  - » Definition of Discretionary – Yes

- Protects Dominion/Control – Yes
- Protects Alter Ego – Yes
- Self-Settled Legislation – Best
- Sole Remedy Charging Order Protection
  - » FLP – Best
  - » LLC – Best
- Migration
  - » Look to Beneficiaries' Resources – Second Restatement Codified

Reference: Which Situs is Best in 2012? By Daniel G. Worthington & Mark Merric; Trust & Estates, January 2012

Appendix D – Using 3DW-TrustSmith.com

For Argonne Trust Company, we have a developed an online application for creating and implementing values-based dynasty trusts. The "3DW-TrustSmith" is designed to help you frame out the values most important to you in a text format. This will provide you and your family the ethos necessary for producing a values-based trust with a legal advisor. The steps include:

a) Use the online "Valgenics" profile tool, which helps to synthesize your core values.

b) Access the "Values Perpetuator" tool, which allows you to select from a list of values—those which you wish to preserve for your heirs.

c) Fill in the "Trust Basics" which will include the following:
   » Grantor(s)
   » Heirs personal data (names and dates of birth)
   » Trust Protector
   » Investment Committee
   » Distribution Committee

d) Your draft document will then be prepared within forty-eight hours for your final approval.

e) Your document receives an "Opinion Letter" from a South Dakota attorney which ratifies its compliance with South Dakota law.

f) Your final trust document is presented to you for execution.

This process can take as little as forty-eight hours and up to two weeks, depending upon your response time.

Appendix E – "Emily's New Shoes"

I presented the true story, "Emily's New Shoes," at the 2008 Million Dollar Round Table conference in Toronto. Below is the transcript from the speech we (Emily and I) made to 8,400 members from all over the world. This dialog was simultaneously translated into 16 languages. The Million Dollar Round Table conference is an international, independent association of more than 38,000 of the world's leading insurance and financial services professionals from more than 450 companies in 80 countries.

Emily enters the stage wearing a new pair of sneakers.

Emily: Hi. I'm Emily. This story started when I read a book my dad wrote entitled "3 Dimensional Wealth." I was a junior in high school when he began writing it. It was the culmination of his lifetime journey that was inspired by the Million Dollar Round Table and its Whole Man concept. I wanted to experience first hand how to create my personal, financial and social wealth in order to make a difference and change the world.

One day as I returned home from school, I read a letter which was written by Greer Kendall, a former Top of the Table member.

In the letter, Greer was asking for donations to buy shoes for the orphans in Zambia. Each pair of shoes was only $4.50, so I decided that I would like to send 100 pairs to Zambia. I waited until dinner to ask my parents if I could buy 100 pairs of shoes.

"100 pair of shoes?" My dad replied. "What do you need with 100 pair of shoes?"

"It's not for me," I responded. "It's for the orphans in Zambia."

"How much are the shoes?" He asked.

"$4.50 a pair."

I watched him do the math in his head. He said, "$450. Is that what you would like to do with your funds?" You see, earlier that year, my dad set up a family foundation and I was given a $500 granting authority for the year.

"Yes, that's what I want to do," I said.

I was so glad that I could actually make this contribution myself. I went online to our family foundation website and sent $450 to "Family Legacy Missions" for 100 pairs of shoes from Emily.

However, merely a financial contribution seemed very one dimensional to me. So, I asked my mom and dad if they thought I could actually go to Africa and personally hand out the shoes. This was a more difficult hurdle to get over. I handled each of my parent's objections one by one and ultimately closed the sale!

I spent two weeks in July with the Zambian orphans. On Day 4 we had "Shoe Day." We handed out shoes to every child, many of whom had never owned a pair of shoes and walked miles in bare feet just to be with us. Experiencing this gave me an entirely new perspective on the cultural difference at home and abroad. What a moving experience.

I remember getting off the plane at Kennedy Airport, my mom and dad were there to greet me. When I saw my dad he said;

Roey enters the stage in a business suit and a new pair of sneakers.

Roey: "How was it?"

Emily: "Best day of my life!"

Roey: "What was?"

Emily: "The day we handed out the shoes."

Roey: The story about the kids receiving their first pair of shoes was unbelievable. But, the real story is not just about how these orphans were changed because of their new shoes; it's also about Emily. Emily has been changed forever. Shoes will come and go, but the heart of one child has been super-sized. For her to understand that one person can make a difference is the best $450 investment that a dad could ever make.

If Emily had asked me for $450 for shoes for the Senior Prom, I probably would have bought them for her. But she didn't; she wanted to give them to others.

Emily's Promise

I met Emily at the airport after her third trip to Africa.

Roey: "Emily, how was it?"

Emily: "Best WEEK of my life. Dad, you really have to come with us next year. I promise, it will change your life!"

Roey: "That's a pretty big promise, but if you're so convinced about it, I'll go with you next year and try to bring the whole family."

Emily's fourth trip, and my first trip to Lusaka, Zambia was long yet non eventful. We joined eighty three other Americans volunteers with the Family Legacy Missions International organization. Our goal for the week was to communicate to the orphans that they are loved, accepted, secure, significant, victorious, and that there is hope for their future.

For five days each of the Diefendorf's worked with 14 to 18 orphans. From day to day, I could actually see the change in

the kids. We spent time with the kids teaching them in small groups and on a one-to-one basis as they shared in depth about their lives, In addition to developing relationships, we asked how we might pray for them.

Roybank is a single orphan whose father was murdered in a witchcraft ritual. When I asked him what he wanted us to pray for, he quickly said, "Pray that our village might change." Throughout the week, Roybank's words continued to haunt me. I also kept thinking about Emily's promise, "this will change your life." But time seemed to be running out for this week to be a life changing event for me.

Day 4 arrived - "Shoe Day." This particular day we gave away 1,000 pair of shoes and over the course of the summer, Family Legacy had orchestrated the distribution of over 7,000 pair of shoes! Having witnessed the joy on the kid's faces, I can understand why Emily said it was the best day of her life.

That afternoon our family took a walking tour of Kalikiliki with our group of 76 kids. The compound was a stroll back in time (2,000 years). Lacking both running water and electricity, the narrow dirt streets were lined with both children and adults. With a 70% unemployment rate, there is virtually nothing to do but "hang out." As our group kids led us from home to home, I could see the reaction of my own family to the horrendous conditions.

Felix is a single orphan whose mother died of AIDS and whose father is the caregiver for him and his 7 brothers and sisters. Felix is the only member of his family to go to school.

However, his education was coming to an end due to lack of finances. My translator, Raphael, told me that Felix's tuition was in arrears. (The semester's tuition due - $6).

Throughout the week, all 76 orphans with whom our family interacted were very excited to tell their friends and family what they had learned. Their friends and family were very interested to hear their stories. But this week's venture into philanthropy was as meaningful for our family as it was for the orphans.

Friday morning approached as 997 orphans, 83 American volunteers, and 120 Zambian volunteers crowded into the make shift auditorium. In the middle of this group of a thousand, a 5 year old girl stepped forward to pray for the Americans.

What I saw was amazing. She had no education, no position, no status, and no power and in her culture, as a female orphan, she has little value. Yet, that day she had a great deal of influence. It hit me like a ton of bricks; that it is not about one's education or position. It's not about one's money and status. But it is about one's heart. I tell you the truth; if you and I would have the heart of a child like this one, we too, would have significance." Right then I realized that Emily's promise to me had been fulfilled - my life HAD been changed by the least likely individual in the whole assembly - a five year old Zambian orphan.

The Kalikiliki Kids

As we said goodbye to "our" kids, we each thought about how the children would be returning to their compound. They just finished the best week of their lives and now would go back to the appalling conditions of Kalikiliki. But our "ad"-venture in philanthropy as a family was just beginning and Roybank's prayers did not go on deaf ears; "Pray that our village might change."

Without the ongoing programs of Family Legacy Missions, we would have left Zambia with heavy hearts, but instead, we left invigorated to "do what we can" as a family.

The Engine that Turns the Crank

One half of the 100 employees of Family Legacy are on the income generation side, while the other half is ministering to the orphans. Here's an example of how it works. A $20,000 contribution will buy a "big" bus. First, it will provide employment for one driver and one conductor. Secondly, the monthly bus revenue will support 12 orphans "3 dimensionally," – personally, financially and socially. Furthermore, additional bus revenue will be put into escrow to purchase a replacement bus when the original bus wears out. In other words, if one capitalizes the children's support, then the support will continue without future contributions.

Let me put this in terms you might understand. It's like buying single premium whole life verses annual renewal term insurance. While the whole life initially requires a greater contribution, the ongoing cost will be eliminated in the future. What a wonderful way to use philanthropy in a creative manner.

When we returned home we met as a family. We prioritized

our gifting and decided to buy a bus, to permanently support 12 kids and provide a monthly stipend for the remaining 64 orphans. Just think about what the next five years might be like in the Kalikiliki compound. Seventy-six kids receiving ample food, medical care with vitamin supplements, continued education, daily discipleship, along with economic development for their care givers. With 50% of the population under the age of 15, the survivors are the future leaders of Zambia. Incidentally, Felix has continued his education and has just completed his first year at the Life Way Boarding School. His life has most definitely changed because of Emily's activities from five years earlier.

So here's the question. Is the Diefendorf family less wealthy or more wealthy by giving away assets to fund the purchase of a bus? Are we less wealthy or more wealthy by spending our "vacation" time and funds to work with the orphans in Zambia? In my opinion, there is no question that the totality of our wealth has been amplified and our "3 dimensional wealth" has been captured and preserved for our children.

I love the MDRT. It is where I learned about the "Whole Man" concept. It is where I learned that giving to and sharing with others increases you as a person. The emphasis on philanthropy through programs like the MDRT Foundation gives us an example to bring back to our families and communities.

So what does this mean for you? I believe that YOU can make a difference. For me it began with a pair of shoes. This journey that my family is on has solidified our core values and unified our philanthropic efforts. It has illustrated to each of my four daughters that "one person can make a difference."

"Who would have thought Emily's shoes would have blossomed into such a life- changing event my whole family?"

Emily: "I did, and it might just start with something as simple as a pair of new shoes for you, too."

Emily Diefendorf graduated from Davidson College, May 2008 and wants to volunteer again this summer in Zambia before starting graduate school in New York.

Monroe Diefendorf, Jr. is a Certified 3 Dimensional Wealth Practitioner in New York. He is the author of "3 Dimensional Wealth: A Radically Sane Perspective on Wealth Management." His "total" wealth management philosophy encompasses not only financial wealth, but personal and social wealth, too.

Appendix F – The Mitt Romney Story

What Mitt Romney's Tax Returns Teach Us About Accumulating Wealth
By James McDonough on October 8, 2012

The **income tax** return information released by Governor and Mrs. Romney (the "Romneys") reveals a well-thought out strategy for transferring wealth to the next generation. Certainly, Governor Romney was successful at Bain Capital and created considerable wealth for himself. What stands out in the eyes of tax advisors is that **the Romney family trust has an estimated one hundred million dollars of assets.** Regardless of your political preference, one must acknowledge the success of a plan that resulted in the transfer of such wealth.

Most readers are familiar with the estate tax, but few are aware that transfers from a grandparent to a grandchild are subject to the Generation Skipping Transfer Tax ("GST") at the highest estate tax rate in effect. Transfers out of trust to a grandchild may also be subject to the GST. Were it not for the GST, the government would not have an effective transfer-tax system, because property could be easily placed out of reach of the estate tax.

Due to the number of topics, this analysis is presented in [to be determined] parts, in order to cover the subject matter in detail.

I. Estate Planning

In 1995, when the Romneys began to execute their plan, they appear to have created a **"dynasty trust."** As we explain below, this is a device to avoid tax. At the time, the estate and gift tax exclusion was $600,000 per individual. Assuming a gift of $1.2 million in 1995, the total in the trust now is about one hundred times the initial amount. One must marvel at the total accumulated. **Estate or gift taxes would have consumed almost one-half of those assets if the plan was not implemented. Instead, all of the future appreciation earned by the trust on its initial corpus escaped estate and gift tax.**

The key is that the Romneys were willing to let go and not have every asset titled in their own names. They were willing to establish and fund a trust and to allow it to participate in good investment opportunities that were presented along the way. Perhaps the biggest obstacle to wealth transfer is the inclination of the individual to retain control. As we can see below, some measure of indirect control may be maintained, but even that is not enough control for some wealthy individuals.

II. Dynasty Trusts

Dynasty trusts are intended to avoid estate and GST taxes. A dynasty trust is designed to allow wealth to pass to two or more generations by eliminating estate (death) tax at each generation. More importantly, by shifting all future appreciation from investments to the trust early on, the Romneys avoided gift tax on the appreciation of the trust assets. One can imagine that this dynasty trust may have been an investor in the Bain Capital's private equity or hedge funds that are, by all reports, extremely successful.

I note that it is often difficult to convince clients to transfer that big opportunity or a crown jewel of the investment portfolio to such a trust. There is a reluctance to give away assets, especially in view of the insecurity caused by the 2008 financial crisis. The tax efficiency of the Romney plan, however, cannot be denied as it has resulted in the transfer of substantial wealth.

The dynasty trust may invest in real estate, portfolio stocks and bonds, or in private equity. The ability of the Trust to attract opportunity, transfer wealth, and minimize risk is enhanced by the size of the assets.

III. Private Equity / Hedge Funds / Alternative Investments

Governor Romney's affiliation with Bain Capital brought opportunities to participate in its private equity and hedge fund investments. Private equity funds are pools of capital received from investors and directed by highly skilled professionals into private businesses at different stages of development. The skill of the professional enables him to achieve a higher return through active management or oversight of the investment. Typically these investments are illiquid, locked-in for five or more years. A typical goal is to achieve capital gain for an individual investor which is taxed at a reduced rate rather than portfolio income. Although the risk is greater, the reward is also much greater than a portfolio stock.

A hedge fund actively trades in financial assets using options, forward contracts, swaps, futures, and a host of other assets in order to achieve a greater return. A hedge fund seeks to exploit anomalies in price to make a profit.

One expects that the Romneys' wealth transfer strategy called for the dynasty trust to participate in some of these ventures. This would explain the significant sum in the dynasty trust estimated to be on hand in less than 20 years of investing. One suspects that all that money was not earned in an index fund.

A reader should understand that the opportunity transferred to the trust could be real estate, a family business, or an intellectual property asset. Stock portfolios that are managed for growth are also suitable candidates.

IV. Grantor Trusts

The Grantor Trust rules were enacted and modified in the years 1924 through 1969. These rules were designed in an era when the income tax rates on trusts were significantly lower than those rates imposed on individuals. Today, the rate structure is reversed but the usefulness of these rules to assist in wealth transfer has taken on a new life. The Service has ruled that a person who is deemed a "grantor" or "owner" of the trust is responsible for income taxes as they are his or her personal obligation. The fact that a grantor is paying income tax on dynasty trust income is not a gift.

When you consider that the dynasty trust is designed not to be included in the Romneys' estates for death tax purposes, you give them the ability to make gifts, in the form of income tax payments that do not reduce their lifetime exclusion. This is, in effect, an unlimited increase in the estate and gift tax exclusion for those who utilize it.

V. Estate Freezes, Discounts and Other Planning

An *estate freeze* operates in a slightly different manner. An asset that is appreciating in value can be sold to family by a Self-Cancelling Installment Note (SCIN) or contributed to a Grantor Retained Annuity Trust (GRAT) in exchange for an annuity. A class of preferred interests can be created in a recapitalization similar in concept to the old preferred stock bailout. It is easy to see that value and opportunity can be transferred in this way for less than one hundred cents on the dollar.

A great deal has been written about family limited partnerships and other closely-held entities (collectively, "FLP") and valuation discounts in the estate and gift tax area. There are numerous cases on the subject which have been covered in the Tax, Trust & Estate News Blog and elsewhere. The essence is that you would not pay full value to become a partner in an FLP if you could not freely transfer the partnership interest, readily trade it on an exchange, or force distributions or FLP liquidation. What is the value of such a partnership interest? It is certainly less than the partner's pro rata percentage of the assets of the FLP. In contrast, if you gave a gift of IBM stock, its fair market value is easily determined. If IBM stock is owned by an FLP, the donee is not receiving stock in a public company but an interest in an entity that is not readily tradable. A former limited partner in the partnership that owned the Yankees said there was nothing more limited than being a limited partner of (the late) George Steinbrenner.

The value of these techniques for wealth accumulation on a multi-generational level is that larger blocks of assets receive professional management. Opportunities can be shifted to FLPs that trustees may be unable or unwilling to take directly. Where control needs to be centralized, it can be maintained by the senior generation in the guise of entity management. The underlying assets are still managed by the investment professionals and business people, but ownership can be transferred without upsetting or changing the structure.

VI. Individual Retirement Accounts

Mr. Romney's IRA provides an opportunity to accumulate ordinary income, tax free, and pass some of it to the next generation. Assume, for a moment, that Gov. Romney were to pass away. He could designate his spouse as the beneficiary, and she could elect to take Minimum Required Distributions (MRD) over her lifetime. The point is that distribution of the entire account can be postponed by the unlimited estate tax marital deduction. When the account passes to a child or children after the death of the spouse, the account may be divided into separate accounts, one for each beneficiary. This would allow the child to use his or her life expectancy to calculate the MRD. The impact of the foregoing is that tax-free compounding continues net of distributions. A traditional IRA earning 6% will have more money in it when the account owner is age 89 than when minimum required distributions began at age 70.5, assuming only the MRD is taken. One should also note that a self-directed IRA may have been used to invest in the opportunities offered by Bain Capital. Although there are restrictions, Governor Romney retained the right to access these investments after leaving Bain Capital, thus freeing him from these restrictions. Today, it is not uncommon for self-directed IRAs to be used by real estate and investment professionals.

Roth IRAs do not require distributions to be taken and offer significant opportunity for deferral. Roth IRAs may hold non-traditional investments that are difficult to value thereby obviating the need for an appraisal each to determine the MRD each year.

VII. Charitable Trusts

Charitable trusts vary in type but offer unique planning opportunities, especially for highly appreciated assets. One significant benefit of a charitable trust is that it may receive a contribution of a highly appreciated asset and sell it without paying income tax. The proceeds of sale can be reinvested. When compared with the alternative of paying income tax up front, the charitable trust option results in a larger sum to invest. Annuity payments to charity are made over a period of years. Payment of the annuity over time will hopefully allow the fund to grow leaving more for the remainder beneficiaries than the alternative of a straight sale. Where the seller needs income, the seller receives the annuity and the charity receives the remainder. Although this is a superficial analysis of charitable trusts, there is much planning opportunity hidden in this thicket.

VIII. Conclusion

One take away from the foregoing is that a great deal of wealth can be passed to the next generation if the transfer occurs before substantial appreciation occurs. A smart man learns from his own mistakes and a wise man learns from the mistakes of others. In this case, a wealthy man (or woman) may learn much from the Romneys.

The above article reprinted with permission from the author, James McDonough.

About the Author: James McDonough serves as Counsel at Lyndhurst, N.J.-based law firm Scarinci Hollenbeck. He has practiced law for thirty years and concentrates on wealth preservation and estate planning for high net worth individuals, closely-held business matters and ownership succession, estate administration and income tax planning. He is also the editor of the Tax, Trust & Estate News Blog. He can be reached at 201-896-4100.

Ownership

If in 1995, Mitt Romney's advisors told him to wait and see what the Estate Tax Exemption would be in the future because "things are unsettled in Congress," he would be paying an additional $17,900,000 in estate taxes today.

The 1995 - Wait & See Approach	Available Estate Tax Exemption	Romney's Actual Growth In Assets	Romney's Federal Estate Taxes
1995	$600,000	$600,000	$ -
2013	$5,250,000	$50,000,000	$17,845,800

Stewardship

However in 1995, Romney took a pro-active approach and set up a dynast trust. By relinquishiung ownership and retaining stewardship, the initial gift of $600,000 into his trust, saved him over $17 million and growing. Incidently, his wife did the same thing in 1995, saving them over $35 million!

The 1995 - Do It Now Approach	Available Estate Tax Exemption	Romney's Dynasty Trust Assets	Romney's Federal Estate Taxes
1995	$600,000	$600,000	$ -
2013	$5,250,000	$50,000,000	$ Zero

Ownership or Stewardship?

As of 2014, you will have the opportunity to put $5,340,000 into a dynasty trust. By embracing the concept of steward-ship, this will eliminate all estate taxes now and in the future (in perpetuity in SD). Following the advice of your "wait & see" advisors may cost your family more than you expect, expecially if your assets grow faster than only 5%.

The 2013 - Wait & See Approach	Available Estate Tax Exemption	Romney's Dynasty Trust Assets	Romney's Federal Estate Taxes
2013	$5,250,000	$50,000,000	$17,900,000

So by taking action 18 years ago, Romney was able to save $17,900,000, and so has his wife for a total of $35,800,000 in estate tax savings.

A NOTE FROM THE AUTHOR

November 2013 will mark the birth of this book, but the gestation period began 10 years ago, and the heavy labor two years ago. However, this journey has brought about another birth.

At the beginning of 2014, Diefendorf Capital will celebrate its 139th anniversary. I originally felt it was my responsibility to perpetuate the Diefendorf name into the fifth and sixth generations, but as I finished the manuscript for this book, it became clear to me that this was not my purpose.

It became apparent during the writing process that the mission of our company is to help clients understand the three dimensions of their wealth and to develop plans to grow in each of these dimensions. What our clients need is not Diefendorf Capital, but rather 3 Dimensional Wealth. In fact, being the best Diefendorf organization is limiting our growth potential. What we are doing is much bigger than Diefendorf.

So with the birth of this book, I will also be launching our new (re-branded old) firm, 3 Dimensional Wealth Advisory. While we will retire the Diefendorf name from our title, we will not abandon the values that have been the guiding light for fifteen decades.

When I am asked who I am and what I do, I no longer will say "I am the CEO of Diefendorf Capital." Instead, I will give this response: "I am Roey Diefendorf, founder of 3 Dimensional Wealth Advisory. Our firm creates, protects and preserves your values and your valuables in perpetuity, in order to help you make a difference in this world."

Story Behind the Book Cover

The cover was inspired by the oil painting below, which was created in 1994 by my uncle, Lee Broglio.

The people in the painting are Monroe Sr., "Poppy," and his grand-daughter, Emily, looking out over the horizon at Wrightsville Beach, North Carolina. It was my great grandmother, Lillian Broglio's, 90th birthday. For five days during the Diefendorf Family Summit, she shared experiences from different eras of her life, which was a wonderful opportunity for her to pass on her values.

3 Dimensionally yours,

Roey

BIBLIOGRAPHY

Buford, Bob, *Halftime: Moving from Success to Significance*, Zondervan, 1995

Gladwell, Malcolm, *David and Goliath*, Little, Brown and Company, 2013

Grubman, James, *www.jamesgrubman.com*

Madden, Robert and Monroe M. Diefendorf, Jr., *3 Dimensional Wealth*, 3 Dimensional Wealth Publishing, 2005

Warnick, John A., *The Purposeful Trust Handbook*, John A. Warnick & The Purposeful Planning Institute, 2013

About Argonne Trust Company

Argonne Trust Company of South Dakota, a subsidiary of Diefendorf Capital, provides corporate protection with the individual attention necessary for "purposeful" planning.

Argonne Trust offers reliable advice and hands-on service to their clients. Argonne Trust completes the service offerings necessary to provide "total" wealth management to families. Through the marketing arm of 3 Dimensional Wealth Family Office Services, Argonne Trust is well positioned to provide the trust administration for creating, protecting, and preserving one's values and valuables - in perpetuity.

503 E. 6th Street, Dell Rapids, South Dakota

ENDORSEMENTS

John A. Warnick
Attorney and the Initiator the Keys of Purposeful Trusts
"Purposeful Trusts are A Better Way. For Trust Creators who want to create a tax-efficient, multi-generational trust which takes advantage of legal choices which weren't even available just a decade or two ago, Roey has created an easy-to-follow roadmap as well as the vehicle to take full advantage of the ride. Roey is a visionary and pioneer of A Better Way in the wealth management and purposeful planning worlds."

Stephen Post
Author
"As a professor in a medical school, I can affirm that Roey has found the medicine to transform lives of success into lives of significance through his values based dynasty trusts."

Jim Stovall
Author, *The Ultimate Gift and The Ultimate Life*
"As someone who has dedicated the majority of my professional

life, through my books and movies, to helping people understand passing along their family heritage and values along with their monetary resources, I am excited that Roey has created a practical guide to making this happen for families everywhere."

Chuck Martin
Author, *Mobile Influence*
"Having been a guest on Roey's "3 Dimensional Wealth" radio show numerous times, I have come to appreciate the real value of values based trusts."

Kevin W. McCarthy
Author, *The On-Purpose Person and The On-Purpose Business Person*
Learning "A Better Way" through the use of a "Purposeful Trust" is eye-opening because it challenges the traditional assumptions in tax and estate planning. Thinking back over my financial planning experiences and education, the valuables, not the values (as the book describes it) have far and away been the primary driver. Professionally, I'm a business designer and strategist who always begins with purpose, vision, mission, and values as the foundation for the business model and plan. The financial planning initiative is no different. Many of his peers may disagree with Roey; but this author has it right. Purposeful trusts truly are "A Better Way."

Robb Musgrave
Author & founder of Valgenics
"Hailing from Australia, I can honestly tell you that values based trust resounds around the globe. This creative planning is a must for thoughtful individuals."

Made in the USA
Charleston, SC
28 December 2013